100 Years of Fashion Illustration

100 Years of Fashion Illustration

Cally Blackman

Laurence King Publishing

Dedicated to my Mother
Jean Stuart-Williams 1920–2006

LAURENCE KING

Copyright © 2007 Central Saint Martins College
of Art & Design, University of the Arts, London.
Published in 2007 by Laurence King Publishing
in association with Central Saint Martins College
of Art & Design.

This book has been produced by Central Saint
Martins Book Creation, Southampton Row, London
WC1B 4AP, UK.

Laurence King Publishing Ltd
361–373 City Road
London, EC1V 1LR
Email: enquiries@laurenceking.co.uk
www.laurenceking.co.uk

A catalogue record for this book is available
from the British Library.

ISBN: 978-1-85669-462-9

Design by David Tanguy, Praliné

Printed in China

Frontispiece: Darani, Madeleine de Rauch,
L'Officiel, 1949. Private Collection.
Photograph © CSM.

CONTENTS

INTRODUCTION

The history of fashion illustration begins in the sixteenth century, when increased exploration and discovery led to a fascination with the dress and costume of the nations of the world. Between 1520 and 1610 more than 200 collections of engravings, etchings or woodcuts were published containing plates of figures wearing clothes peculiar to their nationality and rank. One of the most famous of these, Cesare Vecellio's *De gli habiti antichi et moderni di diverse parti del mondo* (1590), comprised 420 woodcuts depicting dress from Europe, Turkey and the Orient. The second edition, published in 1598, included dress from Africa and Asia as well as 20 plates on New World dress. For centuries, artists had of course depicted clothes, but these early woodcuts were the first dedicated illustrations of dress and, as such, became the prototype for fashion illustration as we know it today.

Wenceslaus Hollar's engravings of mid-seventeenth-century English fashions continued the genre, and from the 1670s onward journals began to be published – particularly in France, by now established as the centre of fashion under the direction of Louis XIV – that could be called the first fashion magazines. *Le Mercure galant* (1672), revamped in 1678 as *Le Nouveau Mercure galant*, contained captioned illustrations of fashion, complete with addresses of suppliers. French fashion plates, the early examples engraved by Jean de St Jean, François Octavien, Antoine Hérisset and Bernard Picart, among others, became the standard by which all others were judged. The proliferation of periodicals, journals and almanacs during the second half of the eighteenth century was a response to an increasingly well-informed, provincial as well as urban, female readership eager for the latest news of fashion. Copies were passed around and shared, while for some women, such as Barbara Johnson, it was a pleasant pastime to create scrapbooks with cut-out plates accompanied by scraps of fabrics and records of purchases.

The industry in France reached its height by the second half of the century with the publication of plates such as those in the *Galeries des modes* (1777), the *Cabinet des modes* (1785) and the *Monument du costume* (1775–83). Many of these plates were published in other countries with text adapted as necessary. As the Revolution ground France to a cultural halt, Germany for a time became the centre of publishing, the *Journal der Luxus und der Moden* (1786–1826) being the best-known fashion publication. In England, Heideloff's exclusive *Gallery of Fashion* (1794) filled the void. *La Belle Assemblée* (1806) and Ackermann's *Repository of the Arts, Literature, Commerce, Manufacturing, Fashion and Politics* (1809–28) were notable journals of the early nineteenth century. The latter, as the title suggests, was a general interest magazine that included fashion, heralding those that became such a feature of later nineteenth-century life. From mid-century onward, France was once again established as the centre

Wenceslaus Hollar, *Winter*, 1643.
Etching. Courtesy the British Museum.

Barbara Johnson, Plate from Album, late 18th/early 19th century. Courtesy V&A Images/Victoria and Albert Museum.

Anais Toudouze (Colin), Plate, 1860s. Courtesy Mary Evans Picture Library.

of the fashionable world, and set the standard for fashion illustration, notably in the work of the talented Colin family in publications such as *Le Follet* (1829), *Le Journal des demoiselles* (1833) and *La Mode illustrée* (1860).

Throughout history many artists have shown a fascination with dress: Dürer, Holbein, Watteau and Ingres all executed exquisite drawings of the fashions of their time. Monet's *Women in a Garden* of 1867, in which all four figures are modelled by his mistress, Camille, betrays a flat, disjointed quality that can be attributed to the influence of fashion plates of the period. Photography, one of the great inventions of the nineteenth century, was generally held responsible for the demise of illustration by the Second World War, yet it too was influenced by fashion illustration, as is demonstrated in early examples by the stiff poses against studio prop backgrounds that mimic those in contemporary plates. Even an avant-garde photographer such as Edward Steichen failed to give as much impact to Poiret's early designs as the innovative illustrators Iribe and Lepape.

By the 1950s fashion editors were investing more of their budgets for editorial spreads in photography. The subsequent promotion of the fashion photographer to celebrity status meant that illustrators had to be content with working on articles for lingerie or accessories, or in advertising campaigns such as those René Gruau did for Christian Dior perfumes. The sixties and seventies were lean times for illustrators, but the eighties saw the beginnings of a renaissance that continues today, a renaissance that has been augmented by the accessibility of computer technology.

Fashion illustration and fashion photography are two distinct disciplines. Although fashion photographers have continually pushed the boundaries of creativity and possibility, they can do no more than record what is there. Illustrators, on the other hand, have the power to select or emphasize a particular feature; to prioritize figure over garment, or garment over figure; to translate a mood, an atmosphere, with humour or emotion, while their ability to communicate a designer's ideas has often led to a close working relationship. And of course they have the ability to invent.

Despite its integral part in the dissemination of fashion, acknowledged since Baudelaire's *flâneur* – the wanderer around the city – walked the streets of nineteenth-century Paris as the ultimate symbol of modernity, and despite the fact that many well-known artists have reflected its cultural and aesthetic power in their work, fashion illustration has often been dismissed as trivial, or at best, a 'Cinderella' art. Falling between fine and commercial art, it has only recently been revaluated as a significant genre in its own right, one that was to reach new heights of sophistication and aesthetic beauty in the twentieth century.

In 1900, when the new century dawned, both fashion illustration and fashion design itself looked backward to the styles of the previous century rather than forward to a vision of the future. Clothing that expressed the opulence of the age, worn by the fashionable aristocratic and wealthy elite of Europe and North America, was informed more by the sinuous aesthetic of the Art Nouveau style, conceived in the 1890s, than by any hint of modernity. The fashionable woman, mature in aspect, was swathed in lace, frills and flounces, accessorized with feather boas and picture hats festooned with bird-of-paradise plumes or flowers, and underpinned by complicated layers of underwear, including the ungainly S-bend corset. Men still adhered to strict codes of dress, regulated by occupation, rank, social occasion and time of day.

As always in high society, dress signified status. Lavish expenditure on clothes epitomized the culture of conspicuous consumption associated with the *Belle Epoque*. Wealthy women patronized the *grands couturiers* of Paris, such as Callot Soeurs, Doucet, Paquin and Worth. In London they patronized Lucile and bought their tailor-mades from long-established firms such as Redfern and Creed. Their husbands were dressed by London tailors whose reputation for immaculate cutting in high-quality cloth was unrivalled.

The less well-off benefited from the enormous advances made in the previous century by the textile and clothing manufacturing industries. Ready-made or semi-made clothing was widely available in the department stores that had sprung up in all major towns and cities since the last quarter of the nineteenth century. Many women employed a dressmaker or made their own clothes: the formulaic and highly detailed fashion illustrations of the time enabled domestic and professional dressmakers to copy the latest designs. Free patterns were included in magazines aimed at this middle market, such as *Weldon's Ladies' Journal* (1879), while Butterick, with branches in London, Paris and New York, had published mail-order patterns since 1866. The dissemination of fashionable styles through the numerous magazines and newspapers aimed at consumers gave everyone the opportunity, if not the means, to engage in the pursuit of fashion.

Early twentieth-century fashion illustration was as aesthetically moribund as fashion itself – statuesque models posed stiffly against fussy studio backgrounds, often framed by ornate arrangements of foliage, known in the trade as 'spinach'. Illustrators working for high-fashion magazines such as American *Vogue* (1892), *Harper's Bazar* (1867) and, in Britain, *The Queen* (1861) adhered to the well-worn tradition of depicting dress in minute, often pedantic, detail, though the work of Adolf Sandoz and Charles Drivon represents notable exceptions. In the United States, Charles Dana Gibson's 'lifestyle' illustrations (rather than dedicated fashion plates) established his 'Gibson Girl' as a fashion icon for modern young women.

1900 – 24

'**Between 1909 and 1929 an explosion of miracles destroyed the old world and made way for the new. ...**' Jean Cocteau, 1957

Louchel, Cover of *La Mode illustrée*, February 1909. CSM Archive.

A ball dress by Alice Blum shows the straighter line and higher waist coming into fashion. The model is almost overwhelmed by the background and surrounding 'spinach'.

Hand-coloured engraved plates were replaced at the end of the nineteenth century by full-colour printing and from the early twentieth century, photography began to make an appearance in magazines. It was Paul Poiret, the most exciting and innovative fashion designer of the prewar years, who elevated both fashion and its representation to the status of art and injected them with a dynamism that made them new and significant forces in the twentieth century.

Poiret established his own couture house in 1903, and his career in the prewar years coincided with radical new directions in art across Europe and beyond. In 1905 Les Fauves exhibited at the Paris Salon d'Automne; in 1907 Picasso's epoch-making painting *Les Demoiselles d'Avignon* heralded the advent of Cubism; and the German Expressionists, the Italian Futurists and the Russian Constructivists explored new concepts and ideologies through art. Fashion is, by definition, modern, so it could not but respond to these powerful new impulses, and during the early years of the twentieth century the interface between fashion, art and design was increasingly reinforced.

When Serge Diaghilev's Ballets Russes, whose 1909 production of *Cleopâtre* featuring exotic sets and costumes by Léon Bakst, exploded on the Parisian stage in an array of dazzling colours and daring nudity, fashion was quick to respond. The pastel shades of the *Belle Epoque* were set aside in favour of a new palette of brilliant hues overlaid with silver and gold. Poiret's designs for eveningwear reflected the oriental influence: harem trousers worn under tunics were accessorized with lamé turbans decorated with feathers and jewels. A tubular, more streamlined silhouette, the *Directoire* style, was developed by many designers; high, boned collars were replaced by low V-necklines; lavishly trimmed picture hats gave way to simpler styles such as the toque; and fussy frills and furbelows were abandoned.

Poiret was a master salesman, but perhaps his greatest gift was as an impresario, linking the worlds of fashion and art by bringing the talents of young artists into his enterprise. Raoul Dufy, for example, designed printed textiles for Poiret's atelier. Recognizing that his radical designs needed a new form of representation, in 1908 Poiret commissioned Paul Iribe to illustrate a promotional publication, *Les Robes de Paul Poiret*. Iribe broke new ground by introducing figures, some in half-profile or even in back view, against sketchy monochrome backgrounds. In 1911 Poiret commissioned Georges Lepape to illustrate his second brochure, *Les Choses de Paul Poiret*. Both these albums, printed on high-quality paper in limited editions, used the pochoir method of printing for the plates. This process, based on Japanese techniques refined by Jean Saudé, involved creating a stencil for each layer of colour, which was then applied by hand; sometimes thirty stages were needed to achieve the freshness of the original illustration.

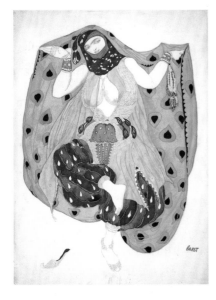

Léon Bakst, Costume design for *Schéhérazade*, 1910. Courtesy The Bridgeman Art Library.

Diaghilev's Ballets Russes caused a sensation in prewar Paris and London. Léon Bakst's exotic costumes had an undeniable impact on the fashionable cultural scene.

Less exclusive and expensive than Poiret's rarefied albums were the numerous new magazines of this period, such as *Modes et manières d'aujourdui* (1912), *Le Journal des dames et des modes* (1912), British *Vogue* (1916), *La Guirlande des mois* (1917), *Falbalas et fanfreluches* (1920), *Art, goût, beauté* (1922), the German *Styl* (1922) and French *Vogue* (1923). However, it was the *Gazette du bon ton* (1912) which represented a unique collaboration between artists, couturiers and publishers. It was founded in Paris by Lucien Vogel, an art director, editor and publisher, who, like Poiret, had the knack of garnering talent. He employed a group of young artists, many of whom trained together at the Ecole des Beaux Arts, and gave them unprecedented freedom in their interpretation of fashion. In a financial collaboration with seven of the major couture houses of the day (Poiret, Chéruit, Doeuillet, Lanvin, Doucet, Redfern and Worth), whose designs were featured in the magazine, the *Gazette* maintained the highest possible standards in content and reproduction. Interspersed with witty text illustrated with *bas-de-page* line drawings, each edition contained up to ten colour pochoir plates and several *croquis,* or design sketches. One of the most influential fashion magazines ever produced, the *Gazette* ran for 69 issues, from 1912 to 1914 and from 1920 to 1925. A special edition was published in France and the United States in 1915, in collaboration with Condé Nast, the publisher of *Vogue*, who went on to buy a controlling interest in the *Gazette* in 1921.

Condé Nast was already investing heavily in illustration for his own publications. Many of the *Gazette*'s original team, such as Pierre Brissaud, André Marty, Charles Martin, George Barbier and Pierre Mourgue, were already working for *Vogue* on all three editions (American, British and French), as well as on other high-quality magazines. Between 1916 and 1939, Georges Lepape did more than 100 covers for *Vogue*. In New York Condé Nast's homegrown illustrators included Helen Dryden, George Plank and Eric (Carl Erickson), whose work had first appeared in the *Gazette* in 1922; while William Randolph Hearst's rival publication, *Harper's Bazar* (renamed *Harper's Bazaar* in 1929), signed an exclusive contract with Erté which lasted from 1915 to 1938, one of the longest collaborations in publishing history.

The progress of fashion was surprisingly little affected by the war, though economic privation, the requirements of outfitting armies, and export restrictions inevitably caused disruption in its production and dissemination. However, many of the Parisian houses continued to hold biannual shows throughout the conflict. For many the war brought new freedoms in dress. More practical styles became a necessity, and for women directly engaged in the war effort – in munitions work, driving or working on the land – trousers and breeches became acceptable for the first time. By 1918, many of the old social hierarchies had collapsed, and fashion began to be increasingly

Paul Iribe, Plate from *Les Robes de Paul Poiret*, 1908. Pochoir print. Courtesy The Stapleton Collection.

Fur-trimmed sleeves and a gold brocade bodice offset the colour of Poiret's evening gown on the left, while the other gown refers more directly to the early 18th-century chemise dress.

democratized. Advances in manufacturing, brought about by the war, made mass-produced clothing more readily available, but for the affluent, postwar woman, Parisian couture retained its desirability.

The modern woman was epitomized by the French designer Gabrielle 'Coco' Chanel, who, having established boutiques in Deauville and Biarritz, launched her first couture collection in 1916, going on to become the most influential designer of the twenties and thirties. Chanel introduced the *garçonne* look: practical styles and easy-to-wear separates in pliable jersey-knit fabrics and tweeds. She also brought into the fashionable female wardrobe for the first time garments adapted from masculine dress, including 'yachting pants' based on sailors' bell-bottoms, and sportswear, featuring her signature knitted cardigans. The suntan and costume jewellery were popularized by her, and in 1921 she launched her famous perfume, Chanel N° 5.

Chanel's exploitation of new or utilitarian fabrics went with innovations in textile manufacture that revolutionized fashion during this period – the synthesis of artificial silk, renamed rayon in 1924, made attractive lingerie and hosiery more available; advances in the manufacture of knitted fabrics and elastic immeasurably enhanced swimwear; and in 1923 the zipper fastener was patented.

The boundaries between formal and informal menswear began to dissolve. Garments such as flannel trousers and blazers became acceptable daywear; stiffened collars were replaced in artistic circles by the soft collar; and the looser, three-piece lounge suit gradually took over from the formal morning or frock coat. Hats remained an essential item, styles ranging from the silk top hat to the felt homburg, straw boater and tweed cap. London tailors still reigned supreme, but US manufacturers began to lead in casual and informal dress. Much of the credit for popularizing American styles and an increased use of colour and pattern must go to the young Prince of Wales (later Edward VIII), a fashion icon of his day, who favoured Fair Isle sweaters, plus-fours, belts instead of braces and checked suits.

For women, the twenties were characterized by simplicity and an emphasis on youthful androgyny, often achieved by using bust flatteners. Low-waisted, tubular evening dresses relied for impact on applied surface decoration – beading and embroidery that reflected the influence of Egyptian decoration (Tutankhamen's tomb had been discovered in 1922) and naive folk-art motifs, while fringing enhanced the motion of popular dances. Neat, head-hugging cloche hats dictated cropped or bobbed hairstyles and became the signature headwear of the twenties. Hemlines wavered: at their shortest, around 1927, they exposed more naked leg than had ever been seen before. The cosmetics industry flourished, their products endorsed in magazine advertisements by society figures, actresses, and that new type of celebrity: the movie star.

Bradley Walker Tomlin, Original illustration for cover of American *Vogue*, 1923. Courtesy The Zahm Collection, Germany.

Tomlin's illustration typifies the 1920s look – a low-waisted tubular dress, caught at the hips with a sash, emphasizes a flat chest and short, bobbed hair. The sunburst, a typical Art Deco motif, is repeated in the elaborately arranged cockade.

Paul Iribe, Plate from *Les Robes de Paul Poiret*, 1908.
Pochoir print. Courtesy The Stapleton Collection.

The vibrant colours of Poiret's *Directoire*-style gowns are
heightened by Iribe's use of a monochrome background.
The deceptively simple layers of the tunic dresses create
a tubular silhouette that is complemented by matching
bandeaux tied round the head *à l'antique*.

Paul Iribe, Plate from *Les Robes de Paul Poiret*, 1908.
Pochoir print. Courtesy V&A Images / Victoria and Albert Museum.

Iribe daringly depicts two of Poiret's dramatic evening coats
from the rear: one embroidered with Eastern motifs and one with
a scalloped fabric feature over the shoulders. The third is lavishly
trimmed with fur.

Anonymous, 'Shopping', *Harrods' Catalogue*, 1909.
Courtesy The Stapleton Collection.

A more realistic depiction of fashionable shoppers in front
of Harrods. A variety of walking dress is worn with large picture
hats trimmed with ribbon, feathers and lace. A new accessory
has appeared – the handbag. The posture of the figures clearly
shows that the S-bend corset is still being worn.

Anonymous, Cover of *Fashions for All*, April 1909.
Courtesy The Stapleton Collection.

Magazines such as this catered for the home dressmaker.
This issue contained six free patterns for garments, including
the tailored separates that were the staple of most middle-
class women's wardrobe.

J. C. Leyendecker, Advertisement for Arrow Collars and Shirts, *c.*1910. Courtesy The Advertising Archives.

Joseph Christian Leyendecker, a German émigré to the USA
in the late 19th century, became one of America's best-known
illustrators. In 1905 he created the 'Arrow Collar Man', one
of the world's most successful advertising images, the male
counterpart of the 'Gibson Girl'.

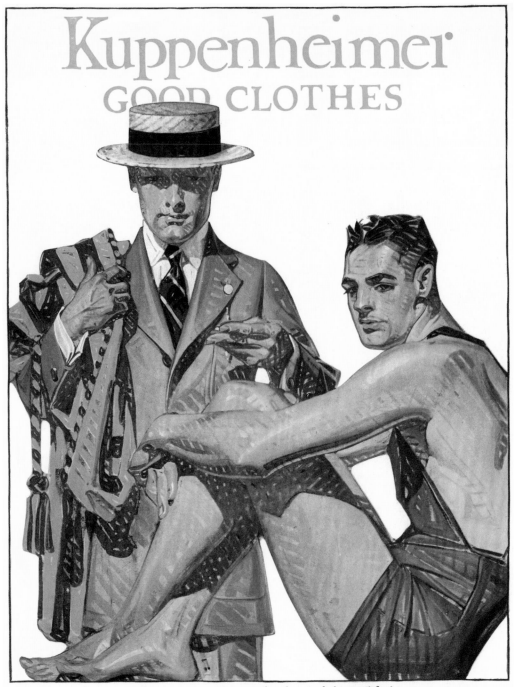

J. C. Leyendecker, Advertisement for Kuppenheimer, 1910/20.
Courtesy The Advertising Archives.

Firms such as Kuppenheimer, a Chicago-based men's clothing
manufacturer, recognized that an artist as gifted as Leyendecker
could transform the fortunes of its business, as he had done
for the Arrow Company.

Léon Bakst, Modern Dress, 'Dione', 1910.
Pencil and watercolour. Courtesy The Bridgeman Art Library.

As well as designing costumes for the Ballets Russes,
Bakst illustrated 'fantasies sur le costume moderne', some
in collaboration with the house of Paquin. The classically
inspired 'Dione' closely resembles Fortuny's 'Delphos' gown,
while the cloak may have been a design by Dufy for Poiret.

Photograph of 'La Perse' by Paul Poiret, 1911.
Courtesy Bibliothèque Nationale de France.

Dufy's woodblock print for Poiret's Persian-style coat,
lavishly trimmed with fur.

C'EST MOI

MANTEAU, DE PAUL POIRET

A. E. Marty, 'C'est Moi', cloak by Paul Poiret, *Gazette du bon ton*, June 1922. Pochoir print. Courtesy The Stapleton Collection.

Marty was one of the original group of young artists, or 'Knights of the Bracelet' as they called themselves, employed by Vogel on the *Gazette*. This much later illustration demonstrates Poiret's continuing use of dramatic effect, which was rapidly becoming outmoded.

Georges Lepape, Plate from *Les Choses de Paul Poiret*, 1911.
Pochoir print. Courtesy The Stapleton Collection.

Lepape's use of a low horizon and flat planes of colour reveal
the influence of Japanese woodblocks (his uncle was the main
dealer in Paris for such prints). Equally innovative are Poiret's
sheath-like gowns.

Georges Lepape, Plate from *Les Choses de Paul Poiret*, 1911.
Pochoir print. Courtesy The Stapleton Collection.

The simplified style used by Lepape may have influenced fashion.
Indeed, he claimed that his wife was responsible for at least
four of the designs in *Les Choses*, demonstrating the sometimes
symbiotic relationship between illustrator and designer.

George Barbier, Fan for Madame Paquin, 1911. Pochoir print with painted silk on reverse, painted bone sticks and guards. Courtesy V&A Images / Victoria and Albert Museum.

Fans were often used as vehicles for advertising. Madame Paquin, a well-established Paris couturier, commissioned a deluxe album, *L'Eventail et la fourrure chez Paquin*, from Paul Iribe in collaboration with Lepape and Barbier.

Georges Lepape, Plate from *Les Choses de Paul Poiret*, 1911. Pochoir print. Courtesy The Stapleton Collection.

Poiret made the turban his signature headwear, inspired by a visit to the Victoria and Albert Museum, London, where he studied Indian examples.

Mela Koehler, Postcard no. 523, 1911. Courtesy MAK: Austrian Museum of Applied Arts / Contemporary Art, Vienna.

The postcard features 'Bergfalter' fabric by Koloman Moser, one of the Wiener Werkstätte group closely associated with Viennese Sezession artist Gustav Klimt. A collective of artists, designers and craftsmen, the Wiener Werkstätte had been founded in 1903 by Moser and the architect Josef Hoffmann. Their philosophy was that 'artistic endeavour should permeate all aspects of everyday life'.

Photograph of 'Bergfalter' dress, 1911. Courtesy MAK: Austrian Museum of Applied Arts / Contemporary Art, Vienna.

An example highlighting the transformative power of fashion illustration. In Koehler's illustration, both garment and model are imbued with an elegance and style that is entirely missing in this photograph.

Eduard Wimmer-Wisgril, Design for a dress, 1912.
Courtesy MAK: Austrian Museum of Applied Arts/
Contemporary Art, Vienna.

Founder of the Wiener Werkstätte fashion department
in 1911, which aimed to combine art and fashion,
Wimmer-Wisgril also designed textiles, postcards,
metalwork, jewellery and bookbinding.

Dagobert Peche, Design for a dress, from portfolio *Viennese Fashion 1914–15*. Coloured linocut. Courtesy MAK: Austrian Museum of Applied Arts / Contemporary Art, Vienna.

Embodying aspects of dress reform as promoted by the Arts and Crafts Movement, and influenced by Poiret's work (he visited Vienna in 1911 and purchased Werkstätte fabrics), the fashion department of the Werkstätte group produced relatively loose 'artistic' clothes. Peche was one of the leading textile designers of the group.

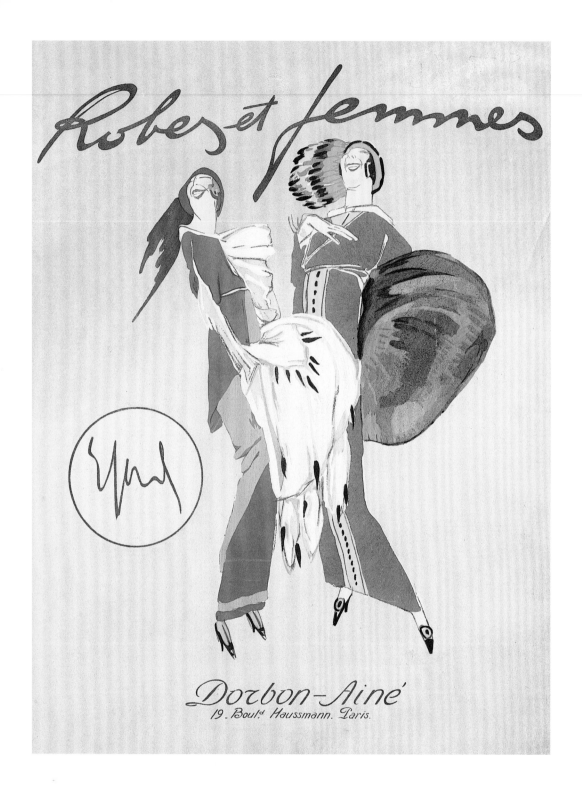

Enrico Sacchetti, Frontispiece of *Robes et femmes*, 1912.
Pochoir print. Courtesy The Stapleton Collection.

Sacchetti, who collaborated with Marinetti, the father of Futurism,
on his magazine *Poesia*, worked as a fashion illustrator in Paris
immediately before the war.

Enrico Sacchetti, *Robes et femmes*, 1912.
Pochoir print. Courtesy The Stapleton Collection.

Here Sacchetti satirizes the fashion victims of the day
and contrasts their overblown style with the easy
elegance introduced by Chanel.

LA FOLIE DU JOUR

Dédié à l'occasion du 1er Janvier 1914 aux Amis du Journal des Dames et des Modes.

George Barbier (above), 'The Madness of the Day', *Journal des dames et des modes*, 1913. Coloured lithograph. Courtesy The Stapleton Collection.

New popular music and dance crazes swept Europe and the USA in the first decade of the century. Ragtime, the turkey trot, the bunny hug and the tango made tea dances all the rage. The American couple Irene and Vernon Castle wowed the nightclubs of Paris and London with their performances. Here a stout dowager looks disapprovingly at the lampshade tunic and exotic turbans worn by the young dancers.

Bernard Boutet de Monvel (right), Plate from *Costumes Parisiens*, 1913. Courtesy The Stapleton Collection.

A three-piece lounge suit with contrasting waistcoat hints at increasing informality. Boutet de Monvel, another member of the artists' group known as the 'Knights of the Bracelet', was himself a renowned dandy.

Tenue du matin

LE COLLIER NOUVEAU

Robe du soir de Paul Poiret

Georges Lepape, 'Le Collier Nouveau', *Gazette du bon ton*, January 1914. Pochoir print. CSM Archive.

Lepape frames Poiret's lampshade tunic and hobble skirt with his signature orange border, painted with a Chinese calligraphy brush.

Photograph of 'Sorbet' by Paul Poiret, 1912. Courtesy V&A Images / Victoria and Albert Museum.

Poiret's lampshade tunic, made of silk chiffon and satin, and embroidered with glass beads, is trimmed with black fox fur and wired to stand out at the hem.

Erté, Two designs for Paul Poiret, 1914. Ink and watercolour.
Courtesy Galerie Bartsch & Chariau, Munich.

After leaving Russia, Erté began his career as a fashion designer
in Paris in 1911. He was soon employed by Poiret, until the
outbreak of the First World War, when he started to illustrate for
Hearst's *Harper's Bazar*, a magazine for which he worked for 22
years. After terminating his contract, he went on to design for the
theatre and for Metro-Goldwyn-Meyer films.

EN TENUE DE PARADE

Robe d'hiver pour la promenade

LES COLCHIQUES

Manteau de voyage de Paquin

Pierre Brissaud, 'En Tenue de Parade', *Gazette du bon ton*, February 1914. Pochoir print. CSM Archive.

A walking costume that directly refers to military uniform, in particular that of the Hungarian Hussars, elements of which, such as the Brandenbourg froggings and fur trim, had entered the fashionable wardrobe in the 18th century.

George Barbier, 'Les Colchiques', *Gazette du bon ton*, January 1914. Pochoir print. CSM Archive.

A whimsical travelling ensemble by Paquin with a cat's-mask helmet. Barbier, another of Vogel's original team at the *Gazette*, was a prolific illustrator. Never as experimental as some of his colleagues, his flat, decorative style was influenced by Persian art.

IL A ÉTÉ PRIMÉ

Robe du soir

Javier Gojé, 'Il a Eté Primé', *Gazette du bon ton*,
March 1914. Pochoir print. CSM Archive.

A satin evening ensemble consisting of a tunic over a skirt
pinned into place with a large cabochon. Gojé was a Spanish
artist who worked in Paris from 1900 and was a regular
contributor to the *Gazette*.

SA LETTRE

Robes de Dœuillet, Beer, Martial et Armand, Beer, Chéruit

Valentine Gross, 'Sa Lettre', *Gazette du bon ton*, 1915.
CSM Archive.

Valentine Gross (Madame Jean Hugo) was also known for her
depictions of the Ballets Russes. Illustration during the war often
reflected current concerns while underlining the desirability
of keeping up appearances. On the right, an elegantly dressed
Parisienne reads a letter from the Front.

NOUS PARTONS

Robes du soir de Premet, Dœuillet, Paquin, Premet, Callot, Jenny

Valentine Gross, 'Nous Partons', *Gazette du bon ton*, 1915.
CSM Archive.

This and the illustration opposite feature the so-called 'war crinoline', a fuller, shorter skirt based on 19th-century styles. Though slightly more practical than the hobble skirt it replaced, it was short-lived.

LA MARSEILLAISE

Etienne Drian, 'La Marseillaise', *Gazette du bon ton*, 1915.
Pochoir print. CSM Archive.

A series of four images with a patriotic theme demonstrates
Drian's superb draughtsmanship. His confident, fluid style in
the tradition of Boldini and Helleu gave his models an elegance
evident throughout his long career.

EN SUIVANT LES OPÉRATIONS

Etienne Drian, 'En suivant les Opérations', *Gazette du bon ton*, 1915. Pochoir print. CSM Archive.

Layered scallops and flounces give volume to the new, shorter skirts.

LE COMMUNIQUÉ

Etienne Drian, 'Le Communiqué', *Gazette du bon ton*, 1915.
Pochoir print. CSM Archive.

In this series, Drian celebrated the innate chic of the Parisienne,
even during times of war. Long overskirts and tunic dresses were
popular during this transitional phase.

BOUQUET TRICOLORE

Etienne Drian, 'Bouquet tricolore', *Gazette du bon ton*, 1915.
Pochoir print. CSM Archive.

Drian also illustrated for *Femina*, *Les Feuillets d'art* and *Harper's
Bazaar*, and for Printemps department store, as well as designing
interiors, stage sets and costumes.

Les Elégances Parisiennes

COSTUMES DE JERSEY

Modèles de Gabrielle Chanel (fig. 157, 158 et 159)

Anonymous, 'Costumes de Jersey' by Chanel, *Les Elégances Parisiennes*, July 1916. Private Collection.

Belted jumper-blouses pulled on over the head and worn over a blouse and skirt typify Chanel's easy-to-wear separates. The centre model is wearing the two-tone shoes that would become a Chanel trademark.

Les Dernières Créations de la Mode

L!HOM (above), 'Les Dernières Créations de la Mode', *Les Elégances Parisiennes*, April 1917. Coloured lithograph. Courtesy The Bridgeman Art Library / Archives Charmet.

Chanel claimed that it was the First World War that made her. Here one of her models is accompanied by a soldier in uniform, while the other male figure wears formal morning dress.

'Sem' (right), 'Coco Chanel as a Milliner', *Le Grand Mode à l'envers*, 1919. Coloured lithograph. Courtesy The Bridgeman Art Library / Private Collection / Archives Charmet.

Originally trained as a milliner, Chanel is caricatured here by Sem (Georges Goursat), whose take on fashion was always humorous.

FROM A PAINTING BY HOWARD GILES

Howard Giles, Cover from *The Ladies' Home Journal*, *c*.1917.
Courtesy The Advertising Archives.

When the USA joined the war in 1917, thousands of 'doughboys'
– men belonging to the American Expeditionary Forces – went
to France. A fashionably dressed young wife bids goodbye
to her husband, who is dressed in khaki uniform with puttees
and a field hat.

From Every Front

—from soldiers fighting in the desperate battles of France and Flanders; beneath the sweltering sun of Palestine and Mesopotamia; amongst the wind-swept Balkan mountains; and in the miasmic depths of African jungle — comes the same consistent story of the perfect protection afforded by The

BURBERRY

Made in Burberry-woven and proofed cloth, it ensures effective security against any wet that falls or wind that blows.

Unlike coats loaded with rubber, oiled-silk or other airtight fabrics, THE BURBERRY is so airylight and faultlessly self-ventilating, that it is as comfortable to wear in hot weather as in cold.

Illustrated Naval or Military Catalogues Post Free.

Officers Under Orders
for France or the Near or Far East can obtain at Burberrys, Uniforms in suitable materials, as well as every detail of dress and equipment.

READY-TO-PUT-ON
Perfect fit is assured, as every garment is made in no less than 55 different sizes. Complete kits to measure in from 2 to 4 days.

Every Burberry garment is labelled "Burberrys."

SERVICE WEATHERPROOFS. During the War BURBERRYS CLEAN AND REPROOF Officers' "Burberrys," Tielockens, Burfrons and Burberry Trench-Warms FREE OF CHARGE.

BURBERRYS
HAYMARKET LONDON
8 & 10 Boul. Malesherbes PARIS ; also Agents

THE 1918 BURBERRY

A New Service Weatherproof

As supplied to His Majesty the King. Combines to perfection the most distinctive qualities of a Burberry Safeguard—double protection over vital areas, resistance to wet and cold, light-weight, self-ventilation, and durability.

Collar can be worn open, closed to the throat, or turned up.

The 1918 Burberry is made in proofed materials, which need no rubber, oiled-silk, or other non-ventilating agent as an aid to their efficiency.

Whilst allowing free circulation of air through the texture, it ensures reliable security against the worst weather.

Naval or Military Catalogue & Patterns Post Free.

Officers' Complete Kits in 2 to 4 Days, or Ready to Put On.

During the War BURBERRYS CLEAN and RE-PROOF Officers' Burberry Weatherproofs FREE OF CHARGE.

Every Burberry Garment *bears this Label.*

The 1918 Burberry

BURBERRYS Haymarket LONDON S.W. 1
Boulevard Malesherbes, PARIS ; also Provincial Agents

Anonymous, Advertisement for Burberrys, London, c.1918.
Courtesy The Advertising Archives.

As this advertisement stresses, the breathable qualities of Burberrys' products made them suitable for all climates. The polar explorers Amundsen, Scott and Shackleton all wore Burberrys' garments during their expeditions.

Anonymous, Advertisement for Burberrys, London, 1918.
Courtesy The Advertising Archives.

Thomas Burberry developed the breathable waterproof fabric 'gabardine' for agricultural workers. In 1901 the company designed a new service uniform for British officers and went on during the First World War to create the invaluable 'trenchcoat', a fashion staple ever since.

Heddi Hirsch, Design for a coat by Wimmer-Wisgrill, 1919.
Watercolour. Courtesy MAK: Austrian Museum of Applied Arts /
Contemporary Art, Vienna.

Early Wiener Werkstätte designs were perceived as too 'artistic'
for general taste. During the war, anti-French feeling encouraged
a self-conscious Austrian aesthetic and more practical ideas,
resulting in the type of warm, comfortable coat with checked lining
that we see here.

Il en est fini des peignoirs blancs que le baigneur se hâtait de passer en sortant du bain. Au bord de la mer, Monsieur aime à flâner dans un -o- -o- -o- peignoir confortable et aux dessins agréables. -o- -o- -o-

MODÈLES DE LA GRANDE MAISON DE BLANC

Jean Dulac, Beachwear from La Grande Maison de Blanc, *Monsieur*, July 1920. Pochoir print. Courtesy The Stapleton Collection.

Two 'Messieurs' draw admiring glances as they appear on the beach in printed, towelling-lined dressing gowns. Swimming costumes were by now more fitted and sleek, improved by elastic and advances in textile technology.

LE BASSIN D'ARGENT
Robe de dîner garnie de ruban

Benito, 'Le Bassin d'Argent', *Gazette du bon ton*, February 1920.
Pochoir print. CSM Archive.

A black satin dinner dress with jade-green fringed ribbons
arranged at the hips to imitate panniers. There was a revival
of interest in 18th-century styles in the 1920s, especially apparent
in the designs of the couturier Jeanne Lanvin. Benito, a Spanish
illustrator influenced by Modigliani, had a long association with
Vogue and did many covers for them in Art Deco style.

BEAULIEU DANS LES FLEURS

Manteau et Robes d'après-midi

Robert Bonfils, 'Beaulieu dans les Fleurs', *Gazette du bon ton*, March 1920. Pochoir print. CSM Archive.

Bonfils' softer, more romantic style pays homage to the appeal of the 18th-century aesthetic.

La belle Torquatienne

Gazette du Bon Ton. — N° 4   Mai 1920. — Pl. 25

Charles Martin, 'La Belle Torquatienne', *Gazette du bon ton*,
May 1920. Pochoir print. Private Collection.

Martin, one of the most Art Deco illustrators on the *Gazette du bon
ton*, went on to work for *Vogue*, *Femina*, *Eve* and *Vanity Fair* until
his death in 1934.

LE MADRAS JAUNE

Coiffure pour le soir

Charles Martin, 'Le Madras Jaune', *Gazette du bon ton*,
January 1920. Pochoir print. CSM Archive.

Martin combines the romantic appeal of distant shores with
a totally modern interpretation. A silk turban for evening wear
is inspired by those worn in Martinique.

CROQUIS
DE
MODES

par

Raoul Dufy

SOIERIES DE BIANCHINI-FÉRIER & CIE

DESSINÉES PAR RAOUL DUFY

Gazette du Bon Ton. — Nº 1   Février 1920. — *Croquis de 1 à VIII*

Raoul Dufy, Title page, 'Croquis de Modes', *Gazette du bon ton*, February 1920. CSM Archive.

Dufy's early career as an illustrator and textile designer began with Poiret in 1911. Shortly after, he became art director for the Lyons silk firm Bianchini-Férier, for which Iribe and Martin also designed.

Raoul Dufy, Croquis from *Gazette du bon ton*, February 1920.
Pochoir print. CSM Archive.

The distinction between artist and fashion designer is blurred
in Dufy's sketches for textile manufacturer Bianchini-Férier.

Pierre Mourgue, Cover of *Monsieur*, October 1921. Colour
lithograph. Courtesy The Stapleton Collection.

Mourgue underlines the urbanity of the menswear in his cover
illustration by setting the figures against a background of
skyscrapers. He frequently travelled to New York and went on
to work for American *Vogue*, for whom he did numerous covers.

AU TENNIS

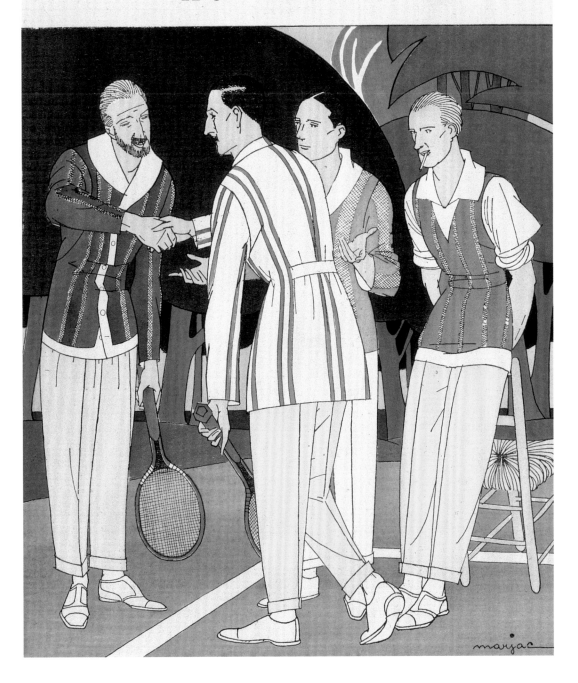

Marjac, 'Tennis Doubles', *Monsieur*, August 1921. Colour
lithograph. Courtesy The Stapleton Collection.

Rodier, a long-established textile manufacturer, teams white
flannels with casual knitwear for tennis. Sportswear, much
of which was made from knitted fabrics, was fast becoming part
of mainstream fashion.

POUR VOYAGER

Si, en temps ordinaire, l'homme soucieux d'élégance se doit d'éviter, en sa tenue, les notes vives. Il est toutefois des circonstances où la fantaisie lui est permise.

Ils composeront des costumes pratiques et bien personnels.

C'est ainsi que, pour le voyage, les complets, manteaux et plaids en "perlaine" par leurs heureuses et originales dispositions de couleurs et de dessins sont indiqués.

(Composition de Marjac.)

TISSUS DE MM. RODIER.

Marjac, 'Pour Voyager', *Monsieur*, October 1921.
Pochoir print. Courtesy The Stapleton Collection.

A marvellously eclectic range of dandyish travelling clothes in tweeds and plaids by Rodier. The tweed cap was an item of working and boys' dress that entered the fashionable male wardrobe.

POUR CHEZ SOI

A chaque heure de la journée correspond un costume approprié. Les robes de chambre qui, durant un temps, ont subi une éclipse, ont retrouvé leur vogue. En voici d'originales :: :: :: :: en " cloky ", légères, chaudes, et agréables à voir. :: :: :: ::

TISSUS DE MM. RODIER.

Marjac, 'Pour Chez Soi', *Monsieur*, November 1921.
Pochoir print. Courtesy The Stapleton Collection.

Startling oriental motifs decorate these dressing gowns.
The caption invokes the 18th century, when such gowns
were frequently worn by men relaxing at home, or even
as informal dress.

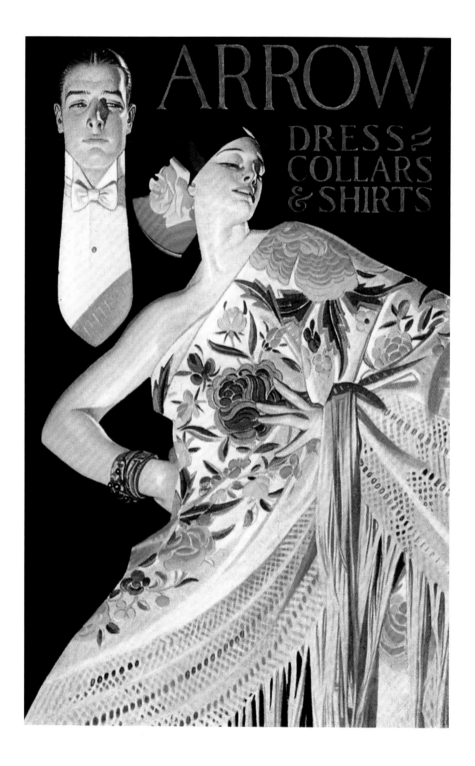

J. C. Leyendecker, Advertisement for Arrow Collars and Shirts, 1920s. Courtesy The Advertising Archives.

Leyendecker continued to work for the Arrow Company until *c.*1930. The starched wing collar and shirt front remained in use as formal dress wear for men until after the Second World War. Embroidered shawls from the Far East were extremely popular accessories during the twenties.

J. C. Leyendecker, Advertisement for Kuppenheimer, Chicago, 1920s. Courtesy The Advertising Archives.

A crisp, double-breasted, wool overcoat worn with a pale homburg hat and walking cane epitomize the dapper man about town.

Helen Dryden, Original illustration for cover of American
Vogue, 1922. Pen and watercolour. Courtesy The Zahm
Collection, Germany.

Dryden was one of the main contributors to American *Vogue* from
1910 until the early 1930s. She also illustrated for some of Nast's
other titles, including *Vanity Fair* and *House and Garden*.

Helen Dryden, Original illustration for cover of American *Vogue*, January 1922. Pen and watercolour. Courtesy The Zahm Collection, Germany.

Dryden's essentially romantic style produced some of the most appealing, yet fantastical, images on *Vogue* covers, frequently depicting imagined rather than realistic representations of dress.

LA PERVENCHE

Llano-Florenz, 'La Pervenche', *Les Feuillets d'art*, 1919/22.
Pochoir print. Courtesy The Stapleton Collection.

Les Feuillets d'art, a joint project between Lucien Vogel and Condé
Nast, appeared intermittently between 1919 and 1922. Published
in English and French, it covered literature and art, though many
of its illustrators, such as Barbier, Lepape, Benito, and Benito's
fellow Spaniard Llano-Florenz, worked in the fashion idiom.

ZWEI SCHWESTERN
ABENDKLEIDER VON HERRMANN GERSON
ZEICHNUNG VON A. OFFTERDINGER

Annie Offterdinger, Plate from *Styl*, January 1922. Pochoir print.
Courtesy The Stapleton Collection.

The German magazine *Styl*, published in Berlin between 1922
and 1924, emulated the luxury French editions with its hand-
coloured plates. Annie Offterdinger depicts two sisters in
Hermann Gerson evening gowns, with that essential accessory,
the ostrich-feather fan.

Krotowski, Plate from *Styl*, January 1922. Pochoir print. Courtesy
The Stapleton Collection.

A shapely three-piece suit with matching overcoat and felt
hat shows the influence of American styling.

R. L. Leonard, Plate from *Styl*, January 1922. Pochoir print.
Courtesy The Stapleton Collection.

Comfortable separates show the widespread influence
of casual wear. For many years, Germany had been at the
forefront of fashion magazine publishing. However, Condé
Nast's German edition of *Vogue*, launched in 1928, lasted
barely a year and with the rise of Nazism, German fashion
became increasingly introspective.

Anonymous, Cover of *Blanco y negro*, 1923.
Courtesy CORBIS/Historical Picture Archive.

The continuing fascination with fashion revivals can be seen
in this outfit, which recalls not only 18th-century styles, but
also the bizarre silhouette of the farthingale, a Spanish fashion
dating from the 16th century.

1922 · 1923

Sonia Delaunay

5

Sonia Delaunay, Fashion drawings, 1922/3. Gouache on paper.
Courtesy V&A Images.

The Russian painter Sonia Delaunay used dress as a medium
for her art, aiming in this way to integrate art into everyday life.
At her Boutique Simultané in Paris she sold garments printed
or embroidered with her colourful Cubist designs, such as these
scarves and hats with abstract patterns.

Ljubov Popova, Original illustration for cover of *Leto*,
Summer 1924. Collage and gouache. Courtesy Galerie
Gmrzynska, Cologne.

As part of their programme of Communist art, the Russian
Constructivists designed futuristic clothing for mass
production, symbolized in this collage by the car.

Alexander Rodchenko, Design for a dress, 1924. Collage and ink on paper. Courtesy Galerie Gmrzynska, Cologne.

This lighthearted design by Rodchenko belies his more serious attempts to create the workers' suit of the future according to Constructivist principles. Such a suit, designed by him in 1922, finally became fashionable when it was adopted by the 'new romantics' in the early 1980s.

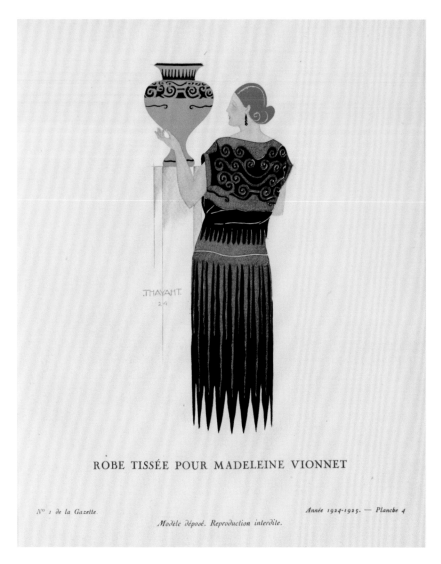

ROBE TISSÉE POUR MADELEINE VIONNET

N° 1 de la Gazette.

Modèle déposé. Reproduction interdite.

Année 1924-1925. — Planche 4

Ernesto Thayaht, 'Robe Tissée' for Madeleine Vionnet, *Gazette du bon ton*, 1924. Pochoir print. Courtesy V&A Images / Victoria and Albert Museum.

Thayaht, an Italian Futurist, illustrated many of Vionnet's designs. However, the use of the word 'pour' in the title implies that he may have had an input in the design itself.

Photograph of an evening gown by Madeleine Vionnet, 1927. Courtesy Kyoto Costume Institute / Photo: Takashi Hatakeyama.

Strikingly similar to Thayaht's illustration, Vionnet's gown is embroidered with gold thread in geometric patterns, showing the influence of the Egyptian aesthetic after the discovery of Tutankhamen's tomb in 1922.

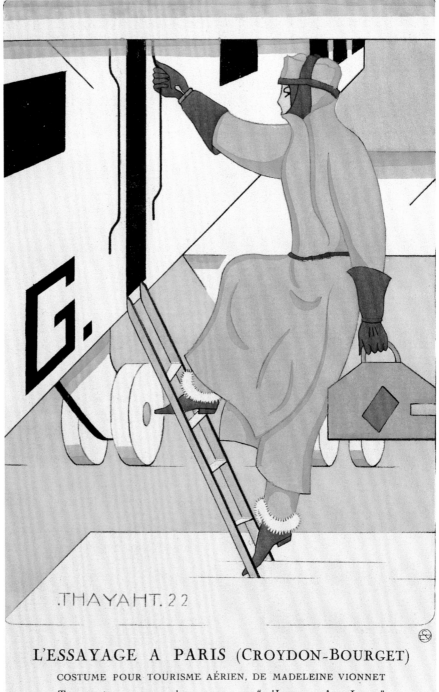

L'ESSAYAGE A PARIS (CROYDON-BOURGET)

COSTUME POUR TOURISME AÉRIEN, DE MADELEINE VIONNET

TRAVERSÉE A BORD D'UN AVION DE " L'INSTONE AIR LINE "

Ernesto Thayaht, 'L'Essayage à Paris', Costume for air travel by Madeleine Vionnet, *Gazette du bon ton*, May 1922. Pochoir print. Courtesy The Stapleton Collection.

Thayaht's illustration commemorates the first flight from Croydon Airport to Le Bourget, Paris. This made a day's shopping in Paris entirely possible from southern England.

In 1925 the Exposition Internationale des Arts Décoratifs, from which the term 'Art Deco' derived, was held in Paris. Notoriously difficult to define, Art Deco initially drew on many of the new artistic 'isms' of the prewar years, went on to encompass the emerging influence of the German Modernists, typified by the work of the Bauhaus designers, and ended in a celebration of sleek, streamlined machine-age Modernism. At the Exposition, Paul Poiret moored three barges on the Seine in which to display his collection, but by now his lavish, exotic creations were increasingly at variance with the modern aesthetic. The *Gazette du bon ton* noted that they were 'the product of a man who revels in the unexpected, producing designs that few people can wear'. Financial difficulties soon beset him; the house closed in 1929, and he was to die forgotten and impoverished.

Chanel maintained her position at the forefront of Parisian couture, launching in 1926 her seminal 'little black dress', described by American *Vogue* as 'The Chanel Ford – the frock that all the world will wear'. Perfectly in tune with the times, she continued to make easy-to-wear day clothes for the woman who desired understated luxury and pared-down simplicity. Sportswear became an essential element of fashion. Jean Patou, whose boutique Au Coin du Sport was the first of its kind, numbered among his clients the ultrachic tennis player Suzanne Lenglen, who, wearing her trademark bandeau and Patou's practical knee-length, pleated, drop-waisted dresses and knitted sweaters, set a new standard of elegance on the court. Sporty yachting trousers with blazers were worn for sailing; skiwear was improved by the use of zip fasteners and newly developed elasticated fabrics, while swimwear, increasingly brief, also benefited from advances in textile technology. Other established Parisian designers such as Lucien Lelong, Jane Regny and Jeanne Lanvin also catered for this market and were soon joined by the Italian Elsa Schiaparelli.

Schiaparelli was Chanel's great rival. Her dazzling career began when her first design, a close-fitting black sweater with a white *trompe l'oeil* bow, was spotted by an American buyer. In 1927 she opened a boutique in Paris called Pour Le Sport, which sold sweaters and sportswear in novel designs. Schiaparelli was closely associated with many artists of her time, including Salvador Dalí, Jean Cocteau and Christian Bérard, all of whom produced designs for her. Greatly influenced by Surrealism, she translated mundane objects into high fashion: lollipop buttons, padlock belt-buckles, balloon-shaped handbags, lamb-chop-shaped hats and suits that resembled chests of drawers. By the thirties Schiaparelli was phenomenally successful. Her philosophy that 'clothes should be architectural; that the body must never be forgotten and it must be used as a frame is used in building' was evident in her shapely waisted suits with squared, padded shoulders that realigned the fashionable silhouette.

> 'Sandwiched between two world wars, between Poiret's harem and Dior's New Look, two women dominated the field of haute couture – Schiaparelli and Chanel.'
>
> **Cecil Beaton**, *The Glass of Fashion*, 1954

Ernst Dryden, Cycling couple, 1930. Courtesy Mary Evans Picture Library / Dryden Collection.

Cycling and hiking were among the sporting activities popular at this time – an open-necked, short-sleeved shirt is teamed with baggy flannels, while a tweed skirt is worn with a short-sleeved top, bandana and beret.

Another couturier whose designs are often compared to architecture was Madeleine Vionnet, the technically brilliant inventor of the bias cut, that sleek, graceful, though unforgiving, style that replaced the figure-concealing tubular dresses of the early twenties. Femininity became fashionable once more – the hemline dropped and there was new emphasis on the waist, now at its natural level, and on the hips and shoulders. Menswear echoed the shapely feminine silhouette: suits were cut with broader shoulders, wider lapels, nipped-in waists and draped trousers with turn-ups. American styling became increasing prevalent, with the US menswear clothing industry specializing in sporty, casual clothing and resortwear. With the increased opportunities for tourism that arrived with air travel, holiday clothing for men was transformed by casual slacks, short-sleeved shirts and streamlined swimwear.

As has often been said, the twenties and thirties represent the 'golden age' of fashion illustration. Condé Nast's admiration for Vogel's *Gazette du bon ton* encouraged him to invest heavily in illustration within the pages of *Vogue*. And from 1910 until the outbreak of the Second World War, its cover – always of greatest impact and importance – featured an illustration by one of his team. *Vogue*'s early illustrators – Helen Dryden, George Wolf Plank, Georges Lepape and J. C. Leyendecker – were joined after the First World War by an influx of Europeans, including Eduardo Benito, Charles Martin, Pierre Brissaud, André Marty and Mario Simon. However, *Vogue*'s prime objective – often expressed by Nast and his indomitable editor-in-chief, Edna Woolman Chase – was to show fashion to their readers in as much informative detail as possible. Here Nast and Chase found themselves at variance with their illustrators, and complained that 'the artists were chiefly interested in achieving amusing drawings and decorative effects ... they were bored to death by anything resembling an obligation to report the spirit of contemporary fashion faithfully'.

Although Nast was keen to promote all that was new in art, as long as it possessed *Vogue*'s intangible chic, he remained ambivalent about the value of illustration over photography. To some extent, his reservations were allayed by the work of the American Carl Erickson (Eric), who was posted to Paris to report on French fashion, along with his arch-rival, Count René Bouët-Willaumez. During the thirties both men, somewhat similar in style, set a new standard of realism in fashion illustration. Their urbane, sophisticated work graced the pages of Nast's publications throughout the interwar years. Already by the beginning of the thirties, however, the balance was beginning to swing in favour of photographic reportage: the first colour cover photograph (by Edward Steichen), of a woman in a bathing suit, appeared in 1932. By 1936 Nast's own analysis of news-stand sales of *Vogue* revealed that photographic covers sold better. As far as he was concerned, the future

Christian Bérard, Original illustration for cover of *Vogue*, 1938. Watercolour and gouache. Courtesy Galerie Bartsch & Chariau, Munich.

The bohemian Christian (Bébé) Bérard, an artist and designer associated with Cocteau, for whom he designed *La Belle et la bête*, was poached from *Harper's Bazaar* by Condé Nast in 1935.

lay in photography, and illustration was mainly relegated to the inside pages.

On both sides of the Atlantic, Parisian couture continued to dominate, led by Chanel, Schiaparelli and Vionnet. But the economic recession that followed the Wall Street Crash of 1929, as well as disputes among French garment workers in the 1930s, began to undermine Paris's hegemony. The US fashion industry, though still paying homage to the French capital, was growing less dependent on it. American garment manufacturers made such great strides during the interwar years, improving large-scale production methods and standardizing sizing, that the US domestic ready-to-wear industry began to outstrip that of any European country. Increasingly, American designers were promoted by major department stores such as Lord & Taylor and Bergdorf Goodman. Hattie Carnegie's smart, tailored suits and Claire McCardell's casual styles, epitomizing the easy-to-wear American look in utilitarian fabrics such as denim, found a new customer base. Wallis Simpson's choice of a gown by the American designer Mainbocher for her wedding to the abdicated Edward VIII further boosted the domestic market.

Hollywood also emerged as an arbiter of style: glamorous stars of the screen, male and female, became fashion icons. Garbo introduced a new masculine severity with her trouser suits, berets and restrained use of makeup. Because costume in film has to have an element of timelessness, given the time lapse between shooting and release, it soon became apparent that Parisian couture dated too quickly. Those couturiers who had been commissioned to design clothes for Hollywood were replaced by inhouse specialists, such as Adrian at Metro-Goldwyn-Meyer and Edith Head at Paramount.

British couture was also establishing itself as a significant force in the interwar years. Norman Hartnell was appointed dressmaker to the British royal family in 1938 and his designs for Queen Elizabeth, later the Queen Mother, embodied the timeless, romantic styles that came to typify royal fashion throughout most of the twentieth century. Other well-known London designers whose work represented 'the English style', based on classic tailoring and romantic gowns, included Victor Stiebel, Edward Molyneux, Digby Morton and Hardy Amies.

Middle-class women relied on skilful dressmakers to interpret the latest couture designs at more affordable prices, while the patterns published by magazines such as *Vogue*, *Woman's Journal* and *Weldon's* were invaluable for the home dressmaker. With the outbreak of the Second World War, these skills assumed a new importance, as women struggled to maintain some level of fashionability in the face of severe shortages and restrictions.

Unlike food rationing, enforced in Britain almost immediately after the declaration of war, clothes rationing was not brought

Anonymous, Advertisement for Dolcis shoes, 1940s. Courtesy Museum of Costume, Bath.

Advertising campaigns during the war concentrated on highlighting the potential glamour of uniform.

in until 1941. In an effort to stabilize prices and equalize availability, coupons were issued for most items of clothing apart from headwear. Fashion houses began to offer remodelling services and those not in uniform were exhorted by the Government to 'make do and mend'. The Utility Clothing Scheme soon followed, involving a range of well-designed, practical and economical clothes and household goods that could be incorporated into the coupon system. In 1942 the first of a series of Civilian Clothing (Restriction) Orders severely curtailed the amount of material used in garments: trimmings, multiple pleats and pockets were limited, as were trouser turn-ups in menswear; surface decoration was forbidden; and there was to be no wasteful cutting of fabric on seam allowances, belts, collars and cuffs. British designers were recruited to demonstrate that Utility clothing need not be unfashionable – within the limitations of the scheme they created smart, neatly tailored, knee-length garments with a narrow silhouette that emphasized wide shoulders and a trim waist, with military detailing such as breast pockets.

In Paris, occupied by the Nazis in June 1940, the couture industry found itself under threat. It was due only to the untiring efforts of Lucien Lelong, the President of the Chambre Syndicale de la Haute Couture, that it survived, though with drastically reduced numbers of houses and skilled hands. The shortages were, if anything, even more severe than those in Britain: fabrics were in extremely short supply and leather virtually unobtainable. Though some couturiers went abroad and some to Vichy France (Chanel retired to the Ritz Hotel, Schiaparelli lectured in the United States), other, younger designers began or continued their careers during the war years, and Jacques Fath, Cristobal Balenciaga, Pierre Balmain and Christian Dior would all contribute towards the successful re-establishment of Parisian couture in the fifties.

It was Dior, however, who provided the impetus for fashion's revival by producing in 1947 his first, groundbreaking collection, the New Look. Having worked as a designer for Robert Piguet and Lucien Lelong, Dior set up his own couture house in late 1946 with backing from Marcel Boussac, head of the Cotton Industry Board. No single designer is ever wholly responsible for innovation in fashion – a fact Dior himself recognized – and the New Look's feminine, curvaceous silhouette was in fact the continuation of an evolution that had already been taking place before the war. Nevertheless, Dior's first collection stunned the fashion world. Its lavish use of fabric and intricate, time-consuming methods of construction outraged those who had undergone – and, in Britain, were still suffering – the privations of rationing. It was in many ways a retrograde style, harking back to the past rather than addressing the future, yet it also symbolized a return to more cheerful, optimistic times.

Eric, New Look model by Christian Dior, British *Vogue*, November 1947. Courtesy The Condé Nast Publications Ltd.

Eric emphasizes the cinched-in waist and padded hips of Dior's coat, worn over a knife-pleated dress.

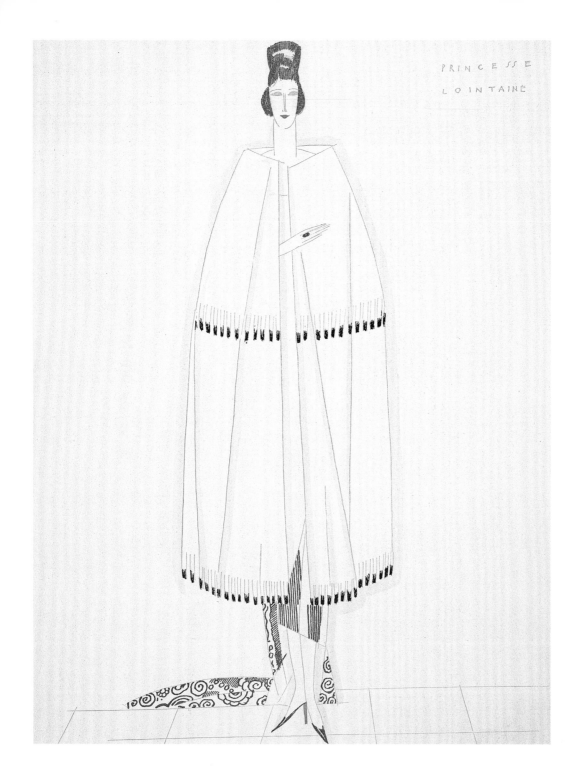

Benito, 'Princess Lointaine', from a brochure advertising
the Maison Fourrures Max, *c.*1925. Courtesy The
Stapleton Collection.

Benito's ultramodern illustrations conjure the exotic appeal
of all things Eastern. The brochure, entitled 'Dernière Lettre
Persane', consisted of 12 plates in 'the Persian taste'.

Benito, 'Schéhérazade', from a brochure advertising the Maison Fourrures Max, *c.*1925. Courtesy The Stapleton Collection.

Furs were extremely popular in the interwar years, especially for eveningwear. Ermine and leopard are depicted by Benito in a flat, stylized manner that utilizes their graphic, rather than tactile, qualities.

George Barbier, 'Winter: Lovers in the Snow', *Twentieth Century France*, 1925. Colour lithograph. Courtesy The Stapleton Collection.

Barbier, who had worked for the *Gazette du bon ton* from the beginning, also designed for the theatre and for film, including Rudolph Valentino's costumes for *Monsieur Beaucaire*. So-called jazz jumpers and Fair Isle sweaters were popular for skiing.

Art - Goût - Beauté

Anonymous, Tennis dress by Patou, *Art, goût, beauté, c.*1925.
Courtesy The Stapleton Collection.

An elegant, dropped-waist, crêpe-de-Chine tennis dress bears
Patou's logo, while the outfit on the left has a relaxed, cardigan-
style jacket.

Anonymous, Informal sports clothes by Patou and Lelong, *Art, goût, beauté*, February 1926. Courtesy The Stapleton Collection.

Co-ordinated separates by two of the Paris designers who specialized in sports and holiday wear. Cruising on the spectacular ocean liners launched between the wars, such as the *Ile de France* and the *Normandie*, became a fashionable pastime for the wealthy.

Anonymous, 'Supercrêpe' underwear by Martial
et Armand, *Art, goût, beauté*, October 1926. Courtesy
The Stapleton Collection.

Lingerie made from silk, crêpe de Chine, satin and lace was
available in a variety of pastel shades. Less costly underwear
was made in the new manmade fibres such as rayon.

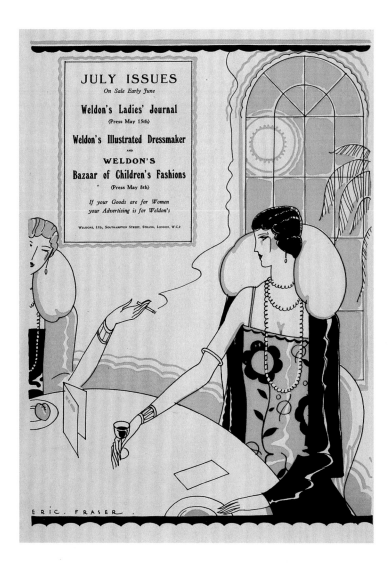

Eric Fraser, Advertisement for *Weldon's* women's journals, July 1926. Colour lithograph. Courtesy V&A Images.

Weldon's Ladies' Journal, from its launch in 1875 until its closure in 1963, supplied the blueprint for the 'home weeklies' that saturated the market during the first half of the 20th century.

Anonymous (right), Advertisement for Harrods. Frontispiece of *Fashion Drawing and Design* by Luie M. Chadwick, 1926. CSM Archive.

A 'practical manual for art students and others', Chadwick's book includes a short history of fashion illustration, technical advice, explanations of printing and colour separation processes, and hints on getting work and meeting briefs. Fashion illustration, at its height during this period, was considered to be a suitable career for young women.

HARRODS

FIG. I. A DESIGN IN FOUR COLOURS FOR COVER OF CATALOGUE

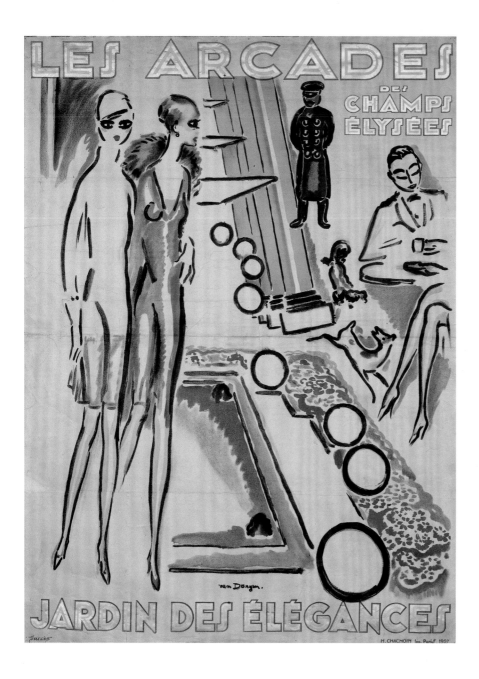

Kees van Dongen, Poster for 'Les Arcades des Champs
Elysées', 1927. Courtesy V&A Images / Victoria and
Albert Museum.

Kees van Dongen, a Dutch artist, became a French citizen
in 1929. His work successively embraced several styles
– Impressionism, Fauvism and Expressionism. His images
of fashionable Parisian life capture *le style moderne* perfectly.

George Wolfe Plank, Cover of American *Vogue*, February 1927.
Colour lithograph. Courtesy The Advertising Archives.

Plank worked for Condé Nast for 15 years, some of them
based in England. Between 1911 and 1927 he did more than
50 covers for American *Vogue*, most depicting imaginary
garments in decorative neo-rococo style.

Ernst Dryden, Sketch for cover of *Die Dame*, 1928. Watercolour.
Courtesy Mary Evans Picture Library / Dryden Collection.

Ernst Dryden's work appeared frequently in top magazines
between the wars, most notably his advertising campaigns for
Jane Regny sportswear. He moved to New York in 1933, and
contributed to *Vogue* editorials.

Ernst Dryden, Cover of *Die Dame*, November 1928. Courtesy
Mary Evans Picture Library / Dryden Collection.

In his final cover version, Dryden captures the tactile qualities
of the fox boa. Applying makeup in public was no longer taboo,
so stylish enamelled and jewelled compacts – highly collectable
today – became a feature of Art Deco design.

J. C. Haramboure, Cover of *Femina*, February 1930.
CSM Archive.

An asymmetrical cloche hat is offset by a luxurious fur collar
and matching cuffs. Haramboure contributed regularly
to *Femina* as well as to *La Femme chic* and *Album du Figaro*.

FOURRURES MAX (A. LEROY)

Pour les Soirs de Gala vos

Manteaux sont aussi Longs que vos Robes.

A droite, une merveilleuse cape d'hermine travaillée en long et dont le bas est légèrement en forme. Deux renards argentés sont placés à l'encolure avec une somptueuse originalité.

L e manteau de tissu, lui aussi, atteint la terre. Celui-ci en velours vert amande est bordé de renard gris. Quelques plis en arrière donnent une ampleur soulignée par la fourrure.

Leon Benigni, Plate from *Femina*, October 1930. CSM Archive.

Grey and silver fox, and ermine, are featured in this illustration, softening the hard lines of the geometric background which utilizes typical Art Deco ziggurat motifs.

Fortunato Depero, Original illustration for American *Vogue*, 1929/30. Watercolour on paper. Courtesy MART: Museo di Arte Moderna e Contemporanea di Trento e Rovereto.

For the Italian Futurists, who advocated 'the overflowing of art into life' and declared that 'our gallery will be the street', the USA was a symbol of modernity. However, Depero, a signatory to the *Manifesto for a Futurist Reconstruction of the Universe* (1915), failed in his attempt to manufacture household furnishings during his time in New York between 1928 and 1930. He resorted instead to fashion illustration and advertising.

Ernst Dryden, Illustration, 1928. Textile collage. Courtesy Mary Evans Picture Library/Dryden Collection.

Dryden uses fabric collage to create an urban landscape that equates fashion with modernity. Spots, stripes and checks harmonize with his chosen imagery.

Porter Woodruff, Evening wraps by Patou and Vionnet,
American *Vogue*, 1929. Courtesy CORBIS.

By the late 1920s hairstyles were at their most masculine.
Here two women sport severe 'Eton crops'. Having reached
their shortest in 1927, hemlines were wavering – a compromise
often involving the use of handkerchief points or asymmetrical
arrangements at the hem. From his base in Paris, Woodruff
reported on the Paris collections for American *Vogue* during
the interwar years.

Douglas Pollard, Black lace dress by Chanel,
American *Vogue*, 1930. Courtesy CORBIS.

A much more realistic style had by now replaced the Art Deco
fantasies of previous years. Pollard was an Englishman who
worked for Condé Nast in New York between the wars.

juillet 1930 **Prix: 6 Frcs.**

femina

Editions Pierre Lafitte *J. Demachy. 3?*

Jacques Demachy, Cover of *Femina*, July 1930. CSM Archive.

A striped vest and beret impart a nautical flavour to this yachting
ensemble. During his long career, Jacques Demachy also
contributed to the *Gazette du bon ton*, *Harper's Bazaar* and *Vogue*.

La Mode et ses Couleurs

Un pyjama en kashabure marine, boutonné sur le côté. Un col en kasha-lisse blanc est traversé par une bande bleue. Couverture frangée en même tissu.

Un costume en flanelle blanche que l'on porte avec un jumper sans man-ches, en jersey marine garni de pois bleu pastel et de fines rayures blanches.

JANE RÉGNY

pyjamas de bateau

J. C. Haramboure, Yachting outfits by Jane Regny, *Femina*,
April 1930. CSM Archive.

A navy 'kashabure' pyjama suit and white flannels by Jane Regny.
Trousers worn by women were fastened at the side until truly
unisex styles arrived in the 1960s.

JEANNE LANVIN

Le nouveau Golf de Deauville, situé au pied de l'hôtel du Golf qu'on aperçoit au fond, est un des coins les plus délicieux de la côte normande. Les jeunes femmes qu'on voit ici ont de charmants costumes de sport de Lanvin. L'un est en jersey marine et djersaspor rayé bleu et blanc, l'autre en djersaspor marron et blanc et jersey blanc.

à Deauville, le Nouveau Golf

Jacques Demachy, Golf wear by Jeanne Lanvin, *Femina*, July 1930. CSM Archive.

Jersey golf costumes cut a dash on the new course at Deauville, 'one of the most delicious corners of the Normandy coast'. Demachy's innovative composition, with the cut-off figure in the foreground, makes full use of the possibilities afforded in the depiction of sport.

Erté, Cover of *Harper's Bazaar*, June 1933. Private Collection.

An orange bathing suit highlights the tan of this mermaid-like figure.
Erté's exclusive contract with *Harper's Bazaar* lasted from 1915
to 1938, during which period he did covers almost monthly.

JANTZEN SUN AND SEA-MATE

THE new Jantzen Sunaire—as modern as this moment! Yes, scarcely more than a brassiere and trunks, but so skillfully styled that it is entirely modest. Extreme chic...yet very practical! Plaited trunks that flare smartly...color harmonies to fulfill every wish, to complement every type. It has the true touch of Jantzen individuality—fitting, as do all Jantzens, as though made for you alone. A worthy beach-mate to the Jantzen Shouldaire which, through an ingenious tie, permits the dropping of the shoulder straps with perfect modesty for an even coat of tan. And for men there's the Speedaire—a suit of marked distinction that offers the utmost in comfort, in sun exposure, in swimming freedom.

F. Clark, Advertisement for Jantzen swimwear, 1931.
Courtesy The Advertising Archives.

Established in 1910, Jantzen was the world's leading swimwear manufacturer by 1930. Knitted fabrics were mixed with rubberized elastic fibres such as Lastex to provide a moulded fit. In 1930 the company developed the 'Shouldaire', a bathing suit with a drawstring above the bust that allowed the shoulder straps to be dropped to achieve an all-over tan.

Swimwear for men consisted of a one-piece suit until the early 1930s, when it became acceptable to bare the chest. In 1929 the Olympic swimmer Johnny Weissmuller (of Tarzan fame), endorsed topless trunks, which he developed with New York underwear manufacturer BVD.

THE SUNAIRE ～ THE SPEEDAIRE

...mbining them all in a fashion ruggedly masculine. Typically Jantzen in its ...rmanent perfect fit, its seasonal style and color leadership, and in the truly ...rvelous elasticity of the Jantzen-stitch. It really is easier to swim in a Jantzen. ... In addition to the Sunaire and the Speedaire, (both illustrated), there are ...ny other smart models for men, women and children...including the popular ...ouldaire, men's and boys' Diving and Speed Suits, and Twosomes for men ...d women. You'll find the famous red Diving Girl emblem on every genuine ...tzen. Your weight is your size. ～ Jantzen Knitting Mills, Portland, Oregon; ...ncouver, Canada; London, England; Sydney, Australia.

Jantzen

The suit that changed bathing to swimming

JANTZEN KNITTING MILLS, (Dept. 104), Portland, Oregon
Please send me style folder in color featuring 1931 models.
Women's ☐   Men's ☐

Name_____

Address_____

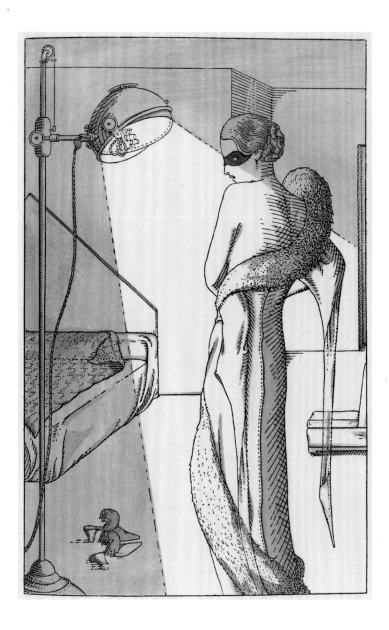

Thomas Lowinsky, 'Clyte abandons the old sun for the new',
from *Modern Nymphs* by Raymond Mortimer, 1930. Hand-coloured
line block. Courtesy V&A Images/Victoria and Albert Museum.

In a reworking of Greek mythology, Lowinsky's Clyte basks
in a pool of artifical sunlight. Sun worship in the 1920s and 1930s
was closely allied to the craze for exercise and diet regimes,
callisthenics and the celebration of the naked form.

Weclawowicz, Cover of *Femina*, August 1931. CSM Archive.

Flared beach-pyjama trousers, worn by a superbly toned model, are teamed with a brief gilet and vest and a broad-brimmed sun hat. Pyjamas were also worn for lounging on informal occasions.

Weclawowicz, Cover of *Femina*, February 1931. CSM Archive.

Like Haramboure and Demachy, Wecla, as he often signed himself, was a frequent contributor to *Femina*. An elegant skiing ensemble is set against a geometric background.

Pierre Mourgue, 'A Saint-Moritz', *Femina*, Christmas 1932.
CSM Archive.

Plus-fours and a short military-style jacket in jersey fabrics
by Rodier are teamed with knitted accessories in this skiing
outfit by Schiaparelli.

René Bouët-Willaumez, Woman in Suzanne Talbot toque hat,
American *Vogue*, 1934. Courtesy CORBIS.

Bouët-Willaumez, along with his rival, Eric, reported for *Vogue*
from Paris until relations became so strained between them that
he was posted to London. However, the two men successfully
introduced a style that was not only aesthetically pleasing,
but also realistic and informative.

René Bouët-Willaumez, La Marquise de Paris in evening
gown by Augustabernard, American *Vogue*, September 1933.
Courtesy CORBIS.

Although the emphasis of the gown is at the back, as was often
the case during the 1930s, Bouët-Willaumez also depicts the front
by posing his model before a mirror – a time-honoured artistic
convention especially useful for the fashion illustrator.

Erté, Cover of *Harper's Bazaar*, May 1933. Private Collection.

The cosmetics industry boomed during the interwar years
and Erté makes full use of the decorative possibilities afforded
by their use.

K. LUKATS K.

Kato Lukats, Showcard for Gré Cosmetics, *c.*1934.
CSM Archive.

Two colours are used to great effect in this showcard
by an Hungarian artist.

Ruth Sigrid Grafstrom, Woman in striped jacket,
American *Vogue*, February 1933. Courtesy CORBIS.

Grafstrom illustrated for *Vogue* throughout the 1930s.
Her painterly style owes much to the influence of Matisse.

Ruth Sigrid Grafstrom, Two women in evening dress,
American *Vogue*, May 1934. Courtesy CORBIS.

Here Grafstrom uses fabric collage to give texture
to her illustration.

Cecil Beaton, Tweed ensembles by Enos and Fortnum
& Mason, British *Vogue*, September 1934. Courtesy CORBIS.

The society photographer Cecil Beaton wrote and illustrated
for *Vogue* from 1926, before going on to become one of its regular
photographers. His illustration was not as successful as his
photographic work, but he was invaluable as an observer and
commentator on the international social scene.

Cecil Beaton, Schiaparelli and Worth evening gowns,
British *Vogue*, February 1934. Courtesy CORBIS.

These gowns show the widening silhouette of the shoulders
already evolving well before the Second World War.
The House of Worth, founded in 1858 by the so-called father
of haute couture, Charles Frederick Worth, continued
to operate until 1952.

René Bouët-Willaumez, Woman in hat by Agnes,
American *Vogue*, August 1935. Courtesy CORBIS.

Bouët-Willaumez was a master of colour, evident in this delicate
illustration of a hat by Agnes, a famous Parisian milliner, which
demonstrates the increasingly exuberant shapes fashionable in
the 1930s. A sable collar completes the ensemble.

Erté, Cover of *Harper's Bazaar*, September 1935.
Private Collection.

Erté's essentially decorative style still finds a place despite
the trend towards realism. Fox fur, leopardskin and astrakhan
are used to great effect in his stylized rendition.

Fashion leaders on the Riviera favor silk net shirts in the new Algerian brown, with half sleeves and open front, worn with light grey shorts and brown and white Norwegian slippers. This outfit is ideal for deck games, luncheon, cocktails, and for wear to and from the cabaña or beach club.

The Mexican poncho, made in lightweight terry cloth and other toweling fabrics in the new reed color, supplants the beach robe. It is ideal for lounging on the beach or for use aboard ship as a robe to be worn on deck. Originally worn at St. Tropez, French Riviera.

At ports of call in the tropics, lightweight suits of silk, linen, Palm Beach cloth and synthetic fabrics are all-important in the new hemp color. This single breasted model is worn with a tan Madras shirt with lounge collar attached, plain color Shantung silk tie, lightweight hose, reverse calf shoes, and Bombay bowler or pith helmet.

A popular outfit at Eden Roc and Cannes last summer was the Algerian brown cabaña coat with carnelian color shorts. Note that the shorts have cuffs like regulation trousers. The sandals are leather blocks in rectangular shape, also making their first appearance on the Riviera.

(For answers to all dress queries, send stamped self-addressed envelope to Esquire Fashion Staff, 366 Madison Ave., N.Y.)

Robert Goodman

SOUTHERN AND CRUISE WEAR

Robert Goodman, Holiday wear for men, *Esquire*, c.1935.
Courtesy The Advertising Archives.

A safari suit worn with pith helmet, bermuda shorts and a Mexican poncho show the multitude of international influences absorbed by the US menswear market before the war. *Esquire*, owned by the Hearst Corporation, was launched in 1933.

Tom Purvis, Advertisement for Austin Reed, Regent Street, London, *c*.1935. Courtesy The Stapleton Collection.

A traditional men's outfitter, Austin Reed opened in the City of London in 1900. Its flagship store in Regent Street, the heart of the West End, was established in the 1920s and is still there today. Purvis's dramatically simplified style was well suited to the requirements of large-scale advertising posters.

Eric, Cover of British *Vogue*, September 1936.
Courtesy The Condé Nast Publications Ltd.

Surrealist-inspired velvet hat and caracul (lambswool) scarf
streaked with blue-green by Schiaparelli. According to Condé
Nast, Eric's work, always drawn from life, 'combined a certain
realism with understanding and conviction in portraying the
spirit of today's elegance'.

Francis Marshall, Portrait of Schiaparelli. Original illustration for British *Vogue*, 1936. Gouache. Courtesy The Zahm Collection, Germany.

Schiaparelli wears a tailored evening suit with military-style embroidery. Marshall, taken on by British *Vogue* in 1928, was an acute observer of British high society and one of the greatest British fashion illustrators.

Marcel Vertès, Couple in a restaurant, American *Vogue*,
March 1936. Courtesy CORBIS.

Where Francis Marshall (previous page) was often gently ironic
in his images of fashionable society, Vertès, an Hungarian émigré
to France, was often more cruel.

Carlos Sàenz de Tejada y de Lezama, 'Cocktail Chic',
Vertice, May 1937. Courtesy Mary Evans Picture Library.

Published between 1937 and 1946, the right-wing Spanish
magazine *Vertice* reflected Nationalist views. De Tejada worked
in Paris between 1926 and 1935, contributing to *Femina* and
Vogue, before returning to Spain.

Carlos Sàenz de Tejada y de Lezama, 'Dog-walking Chic',
Vertice, May 1937. Courtesy Mary Evans Picture Library.

These middle-market styles do not reflect the verve of Spain's
most significant contribution to fashion in the mid-20th century:
the designer Balenciaga, who left Spain at the outbreak of the
Civil War and showed his first Paris collection in 1937.

Christian Bérard, Chanel designs, *Vogue*, July 1937. Courtesy V&A Images / Victoria and Albert Museum.

'Chanel dines at home in printed pyjamas, sweater and barbaric jewels. ...' Coco Chanel epitomized the modern woman in her life as well as her work. Trousers, here worn for the evening, were one example of the many garments she adapted from the male wardrobe.

Christian Bérard, Schiaparelli designs, *Vogue*, October 1938. Courtesy V&A Images / Victoria and Albert Museum.

Surrealist imagery is embroidered onto Schiaparelli's evening cape. In the late 1930s she launched a series of themed collections, including the Astrological collection from which these models derive.

Georges Lepape, Cover design for French and British *Vogue*, 1938. Pencil. Courtesy Galerie Bartsch & Chariau, Munich.

Lepape's last cover for *Vogue* brought to an end an association that lasted 22 years and included over 80 covers. The figure was eventually modelled in plaster and photographed against a realistic background, perhaps signalling Lepape's acknowledgement of the growing supremacy of that medium.

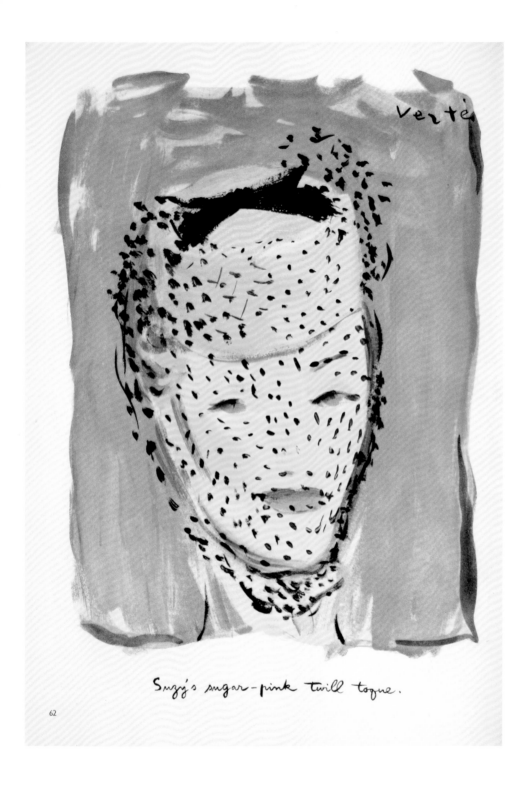

Verté

Suzy's sugar-pink twill toque.

62

Marcel Vertès, Suzy toque, *Harper's Bazaar*, June 1938.
Private Collection.

When not indulging in caricature, Vertès could produce charming
work, as in this depiction of a sugar-pink toque with a spotted
black veil.

Marcel Vertès, Reboux bonnet, *Harper's Bazaar*, June 1938.
Private Collection.

A bonnet by Reboux with cornflowers filling the brim at the front
and a halo of dark-blue straw at the back. In the early 1940s
Vertès moved to the USA.

Hof, Men's evening suits by Simpson's, 1938. Courtesy Museum
of Costume, Bath.

Formal wear for men still required either a dinner jacket,
worn here with a soft-collared shirt and black tie, or a tailcoat,
worn with white tie, waistcoat and stiff collar.

Hemjic, Advertisement for Olympic's 'Rockfeller' suit.
Courtesy The Stapleton Collection.

The wider American cut of informal suits for men was generally
adopted by the late 1930s. Broad-shouldered, and close-fitting
over the waist and hips, the jacket was worn with loose, draped
trousers with turn-ups. A grey fedora hat completes the outfit.

Matching the hatband, the lipstick and nail varnish that Cyclax call " Brilliant."

Marcel Vertès, Hat, *Harper's Bazaar*, March 1940.
Private Collection.

Makeup becomes increasingly important during wartime.
Cyclax's 'Brilliant' lipstick and nail varnish are deemed
suitable for welcoming home the husband on leave.

Yellow is starred by Molyneux
throughout his collection.   A lovely clear
yellow that needs the fresh
bright makeup of Elizabeth
Arden called Primula.

Pierre Mourgue, Molyneux evening gown, *Harper's Bazaar*,
June 1940. Private Collection.

Elizabeth Arden's 'Primula' makeup complements Molyneux's
sari-style evening gown. English-born Captain Edward Molyneux
was an important designer during the 1930s, with houses
in both London and Paris. During the war he was one of the
designers commissioned by the Board of Trade to promote
the Utility scheme.

Anonymous, Twinset and tweed skirt by Harrods, 1939/40.
Courtesy Museum of Costume, Bath.

With the outbreak of the Second World War, the English style was
readily adapted to the practical requirements of wartime clothing.
The turban-like scarf tied round the head was an informal
alternative to a hat.

Herbert Mocho, Design for a suit, *Berliner Mode*, Winter 1940.
Courtesy BPK Berlin.

While in Germany Paris fashion was dismissed as 'degenerate',
'unpatriotic' and a threat to the 'true German look', it was
nevertheless eagerly consumed by those who could obtain it.
The Occupation of Paris meant that much of the couture output
was directed towards Germany.

Anonymous, Designs from *Berliner Mode*, Spring 1940.
Courtesy BPK Berlin.

During the war, clothes rationing in Germany was as strict
as in other countries. The 'Aryanization' of the domestic fashion
industry, largely dependent on a Jewish workforce, resulted
in its almost complete collapse.

Anonymous, Designs from *Berliner Mode*, Summer 1941.
Courtesy BPK Berlin.

Summer fashions hint at the patriotic dirndl skirt shape promoted
by the Nazis. Wood- or cork-soled shoes became an economic
necessity due to the shortage of leather.

Francis Marshall, 'Taping the Windows', *c*.1939, from *London West*, 1944. Private Collection.

Published in 1944, Marshall's book *London West* is a unique record of society life in London during the 1930s, up to and including the early war years. Marshall served in the navy during the war while continuing to illustrate for *Vogue*.

Tea in the hall, blitz style

Francis Marshall, 'Tea in the Blitz', 1941, from *London West*,
1944. Private Collection.

The newspaper headline shows that this drawing was done
in 1941 during the height of the Blitz. Sudden air-raid warnings
meant that the dress code for the shelters was 'come as you are'.

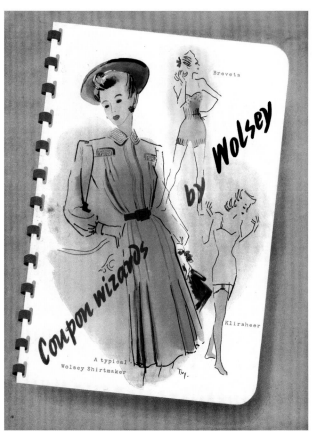

Donia Nachshen, 'Go through your Wardrobe', from *Make Do and Mend*, 1940s. Courtesy The Advertising Archives.

The 'Make Do and Mend' campaign booklets were prepared for the Board of Trade and published by the Ministry of Information. They were packed with useful tips on mending, renovating and caring for clothes.

T. W., Advertisement for Wolsey, 1940s. Courtesy The Advertising Archives.

Founded in the mid-18th century in Leicester, Wolsey started as an hosiery and underwear manufacturer. The square shoulders, short skirt and economical use of fabric in the 'shirtmaker' are typical of rationed fashion.

Anonymous, Advertisement for Elizabeth Arden, 1940s.
Courtesy The Advertising Archives.

Cosmetics and patriotism are conflated in this advertisement.
Because many of the base ingredients for cosmetics were needed
for war purposes, makeup was in short supply. Women showed
great ingenuity, the most famous example being that of painting
a faux seam down the back of the legs to resemble stockings.

Hof, Advertisement for Yardley, 1940s. Courtesy The
Advertising Archives.

Yardley stresses the importance of keeping up morale
by looking one's best, despite the less attractive qualities
of wartime packaging.

Eric, Advertisement for L. S. Ayres & Co. of Indianapolis, 1942. Private Collection.

Eric's drawing of a belted suit with a gathered peplum hints at the style of the New Look to come.

Ruth Sigrid Grafstrom, Advertisement for Flexees Combinations and Girdles, 1942. Private Collection.

Declaring that 'Fashion-wise women know that any costume is only as smart as its foundation', the advertisement stresses the importance of boosting the morale of the soldier on leave. A box at the bottom advertises war bonds and stamps.

R. S., Advertisement for Lee Jeans, 1943. Courtesy
The Advertising Archives.

The USA joined the war after the bombing of Pearl Harbor
in 1941. Garment manufacturers, as is stressed in this
advertisement, had to put the requirements of outfitting the
army first, but denim jeans, worn by blue-collar workers since
the 19th century, were about to enter the fashion arena.

Rivett, Advertisement for Harella, London, 1940s.
Courtesy The Advertising Archives.

The dream-like imagery of Surrealism is invoked
by a photomontage depicting a sensible double-breasted
overcoat with padded shoulders, against a background
of architecture and a figure of Britannia in a glass case.

It's a dream... it's HARELLA

Exhibition of combined operations by Harella — a treasure of a utility coat, light as cloud, warm as sunshine and flattering as a compliment, in fleecy dove-beige Alpaca mixture, fully lined crepe, 102/10d ; combined with a tailored utility suit of pure West of England wool (in many colourful checks) 92/10d. See both, together with many other triumphant Harella 'couples' at any good fashion store; or if in any difficulty write to the Harella Showrooms, 243 Regent Street, London, W.1. (Wholesale only.)

F.H.K. Henrion, Advertisement for Harella, London, 1940s.
Courtesy The Advertising Archives.

Using wartime terminology, the caption describes a Utility alpaca coat and wool suit set against the backdrop of the 1851 Great Exhibition at Crystal Palace, juxtaposed with parachuting figures and Punch. Born in Germany, Henrion adopted British nationality in 1946.

Jacques Demachy, Hat by Paulette, 1943. Mixed media.
Courtesy The Zahm Collection, Germany.

Hats were the main outlet of fashionable expression in wartime
Paris. A confection of feathers, net and flowers set at the front
of the head defies the dowdiness of war.

Pierre Louchel, Woman in suit, 1943. Ink and watercolour.
Courtesy The Zahm Collection, Germany.

As in Germany, a shortage of leather brought about new styles
in footwear – here platform-soled shoes, possibly using wood
or cork, are worn with a smart tailored suit and a hat with a snood.
After the Liberation of France in 1944, chronic shortages
of textiles and cosmetics continued.

Anonymous, Advertisement for the Art Institute of Pittsburgh, *c.*1944. Courtesy CORBIS/Lake County Museum.

Fashion illustration was still an integral part of some fashion design courses at art colleges. Unless employed as a staff illustrator for a publication or by a department store, an illustrator was likely to be freelance. This afforded women the opportunity to combine working from home with a family.

"Really Tailored" Clothes

S.H. CHURCHILL & CO.
CHICAGO 7, ILL.

Anonymous, Advertisement for Churchill tailoring, *c.*1944.
Courtesy CORBIS/Lake County Museum.

Tailored clothes by Churchill of Chicago were given extra
cachet by association with Britain's iconic wartime leader.

Anonymous, Advertisement for Panda Footwear, 1940s.
Courtesy The Stapleton Collection.

A glamorous couple walk past a flower seller, still a favourite
figure in depictions of London street scenes.

Within the advertisement image:

for such a lovely Gift.
And this is what I
have bought with it – a
pair of 'CORVETTE' shoes made
by PANDA – just the shoes
you would want me to
have if you were here

Panda
Co-eds

At the leading stores and
shoe shops in various colours
of suede and calf.

'Corvette'

THE PANDA FOOTWEAR COMPANY, LIMITED, FLEMPTON ROAD, LEYTON, LONDON, E.10

Anonymous, Advertisement for Panda Footwear, 1940s.
Courtesy The Stapleton Collection.

A pair of 'Corvette' co-eds, named after a type of battleship,
is gratefully purchased with a gift of money or coupons.

MOLYNEUX
TISSU LESUR

17

Alexandre Delfau, Molyneux dress and leopard coat, *La Femme chic*, Spring 1945. Private Collection.

Known for his reliably elegant clothes, Molyneux's long career started in London with Lucile.

Alexandre Delfau, Winter outfits by Balenciaga, *Plaire*, Vol. II, 1945. Courtesy V&A Images / Victoria and Albert Museum.

Balenciaga, one of the most admired couturiers in Paris from 1937 until his retirement in 1968, hints at the new silhouette, distilled by Dior in his 1947 collection.

Francis Marshall, Advertisement for Jaeger, 1945. Courtesy
The Advertising Archives.

Peace brought with it a new optimism. Long hair, modelled on
styles worn by movie stars such as Gloria Swanson and Veronica
Lake, was now fashionable and trousers – or 'slacks' as they
were more commonly known – had finally been accepted as more
than mere workwear or sportswear.

PERFECTION in dress and economy are best served by selecting suitings that after long use show little signs of wear.

A suit of such cloth made by an expert tailor is astonishing in distinction of excellence throughout a long life.

A long life is very desirable to-day. The more reason then that the suit is one that will please and neither tire nor annoy its owner in any way. Texture, pattern and particularly fitting must all appeal and continue to satisfy.

Burberrys can be relied upon to supply the above essentials.

Telephone :
Whitehall 3343

BURBERRYS
HAYMARKET LONDON S.W.I
BURBERRYS LTD.

Anonymous, Advertisement for Burberrys, 1945. Courtesy The Advertising Archives.

At the end of the war, the Government-issue 'demob' suit had to suffice for many men, while those who could afford it returned to tailoring firms like Burberrys. Little has changed in terms of style between this example and suits worn before the war.

Reading from left to right—

Perfect complement for your suit or odd skirt—full-sleeved shirt in soft wool. Note the new right-hand flap pocket. Black, blue, yellow, brown, royal, red. (6 *coupons*). **£3.5.0**

Fine jersey blouse with high-fitting collar and fulness gathered into shoulder yoke. Cherry red, royal, brown, black, tan, navy, and sky. (6 *coupons*). **£3.9.6**

Pleats to the fore, panelled back, three-button fastening to the skirt of this *tailleur* in check suiting. Self buttons to jacket. In heather, over-checked royal or green. Hips 36-44 inches. (18 *coupons*). **£13.3.9**

Reversing the order—pleats to the back, plain front, three-button fastening to the skirt. Bias yoke to jacket. Green/brown, blue/brown, or heather/brown. Hips 36-40 inches. (18 *coupons*). **£12.6.2**

HARRODS LTD

Colour—the Keynote of the New Blouses & Suits

LONDON SW1

Anonymous, Advertisement for Harrods, 1940s.
Courtesy The Stapleton Collection.

Clothing rationing lasted in Britain until 1949. In 1945, 48 coupons per person were issued.

Anonymous, 'New York by Starlight', *Woman's Journal*, July 1946. Courtesy Museum of Costume, Bath.

Dinner and dance dresses by some of the USA's leading designers, including Hattie Carnegie, Adele Simpson, Nettie Rosenstein and Muriel King. During the war, in the absence of Parisian couture, the domestic industry had started to promote its own designers.

Christian Bérard (left), 'Bar', from Christian Dior's New Look collection, 1947. Watercolour. Courtesy Archives Christian Dior, Paris.

The 'Bar' ensemble was the keynote design of Dior's 'New Look' collection (so called by Carmel Snow, *Harper's Bazaar*'s influential editor), launched in 1947. A gently padded jacket with a tiny fitted waist is worn over a full, pleated skirt and balanced by a straw 'coolie' hat. Bérard was a close friend of Dior's and advised him on the interior decoration of his first salon at 30 avenue Montaigne.

Photograph of 'Bar', 1947. Courtesy V&A Images / Victoria and Albert Museum. Photographer: Willy Maywald.

An example of how a photographed garment can appear to be less appealing than the illustrated version, despite the elegant pose of the model.

René Gruau, Original illustration of 'Bar' for German *Vogue*, 1966.
Ink and gouache. Courtesy Galerie Bartsch & Chariau, Munich.

Twenty years after its creation, Dior's 'Bar' ensemble is given
a modern interpretation in Gruau's dynamic drawing and looks
as elegant as ever.

Eric, Original illustration for British *Vogue*, November 1947.
Watercolour. Courtesy Galerie Bartsch & Chariau, Munich.

Lucien Lelong's wool suit typifies an alternative, less extravagant
silhouette to Dior's New Look, though this does not prevent
disparaging glances from bystanders.

Two very different silhouettes are outstanding in Paris for day-time wear this winter. One shows a full pleated ballet-length skirt topped by a loose raglan-shouldered jacket which follows the same wide line, and is illustrated in Dior's black tiny-waisted wool frock with the red, white and black tartan jacket lined with black seal. The other emphasises the draped Magyar sleeved jacket above a slender, almost hobble skirt, as in Lelong's off-white velour-cloth dress and cape-jacket trimmed with mink. In both cases shoulders are narrow and rounded, collars outstanding, waists are tightly nipped-in, and skirts are mid-calf length.

Listen for the swish of duchess satin this afternoon. It begins in the afternoon with a dress as subtly provocative as Dior's model in oyster-pink, the full ballet skirt widening the hips with looped pleats under a draped corselet waist, and completely belying the prim, turn-of-the-century look of the fitted bodice with its military collar and long Magyar sleeves. Neat little basqued jackets over immensely full skirts are favoured for evening, contrasting the dark on the light, the dull on the gleaming, as shown in Piguet's dinner dress with the tortoise-shell brown duchess satin skirt beneath a black jacket of matt woollen which is fringed and embroidered with black sequins.

Christian Dior

Lucien Lelong

Christian Dior

Robert Piguet

Reproduction Interdite

René Gruau, Paris Collections, *Woman's Journal*, 1947. Courtesy Museum of Costume, Bath.

Dior launched a second New Look collection in the autumn of 1947. His models, first and third from left, are shown alongside Lucien Lelong's and Robert Piguet's. Lelong's (second from left) offers an alternative silhouette, with a pencil-thin skirt.

Far left—An afternoon dress of soft crepe, whose horizontal print is used with originality to minimise your waist. The bodice is caught up in soft folds—the skirt, with its moulded hip line is enriched with a swirl of pleats. Red or navy grounds with grey and white. Hips 35–40. 7 coupons.

£17 6 0

Left—Summer elegance in an exquisite print jumper suit for all occasions. Note the flattering neckline, the new hip movement, the swinging skirt and the feminine touch of butterfly bows. Light or dark grounds. Hips 35-40. 8 coupons. £17 6 0

Personal Shoppers only

Younger Set Gowns — First Floor

HARRODS

HARRODS LTD

LONDON SW1

Anonymous, *Harrods summer dresses, 1940s.* Courtesy
The Stapleton Collection.

The influence of the New Look can clearly be seen in these
printed summer dresses from Harrods, still requiring coupons.

René Gruau, Original illustration of Christian Dior for cover
of *L'Officiel*, October 1948. Brush drawing in ink, watercolour
and gouache. Courtesy Galerie Bartsch & Chariau.

Gruau's work dominates the high-fashion magazines of the
1950s. His decisive, graphic outline always produced a dramatic
effect. He was Dior's favourite illustrator; their association began
before the war when they worked together on the newspaper
Le Figaro.

René Gruau, Ensemble by Christian Dior, *Femina*, IV, 1949.
Courtesy Museum of Costume, Bath.

Dior deplored the demise of the hat, which he attributed
to a reaction against those worn during the war. For him,
a woman was not properly dressed without one.

René Gruau, Original illustration for *Adam*, 1948/9.
Brush drawing and watercolour. Courtesy Galerie Bartsch
& Chariau, Munich.

In a sharply tailored suit, a model poses with the hauteur
that was to become typical of 1950s fashion images.

Darani, Madeleine de Rauch, *L'Officiel*, 1949.
Private Collection.

An astonishingly modern image – a yellow wool
jacket and checked trousers (now entering couture)
for weekend wear.

Tom Keogh, Costume design for Gladys Cooper, 1948/50.
Ink and watercolour. Courtesy Galerie Bartsch & Chariau, Munich.

Many illustrators moved effortlessly between the world
of fashion and the stage or cinema. Keogh, an American,
designed costumes for Marlene Dietrich, Mae West and Gladys
Cooper, a major British actress during the 1940s. This design
may well have been for Cooper's role as Aunt Inez in Vincente
Minnelli's film *The Pirate*, 1948.

Tom Keogh, Fashion drawing for French *Vogue*, *c*.1950.
Ink and watercolour. Courtesy Galerie Bartsch & Chariau, Munich.

As well as contributing regularly to French *Vogue* between
1947 and 1951, Keogh illustrated novels written by his wife,
Theodora Keogh.

Tod Draz, Original illustration for American *Vogue*, August
1950. Crayon and watercolour. Courtesy Galerie Bartsch
& Chariau, Munich.

A head-hugging cloche hat with turned-back brim by Draz,
an American illustrator featured in British and French *Vogue*,
the *New York Times* and *International Textiles*. His later style
was more impressionistic, with less firm draughtsmanship.

Bernard Blossac, Original illustration for hat by Legroux for French *Vogue*, 1950. Pencil and watercolour. Courtesy Galerie Bartsch & Chariau, Munich.

Hats such as this one shaped like flying saucers balanced the wide skirts of the New Look.

René Gruau, Original illustration for *International Textiles*,
April 1951. Collection of The Gemeentemuseum Den Haag.

Like Lepape, Gruau often used a framing device in his drawings.
His elegant outline gives impact to the narrow line that ran
in tandem with the wide-skirted New Look silhouette.

René Gruau, Original illustration for *International Textiles*,
April 1951. Collection of The Gemeentemuseum Den Haag.

Published monthly in Holland from 1933 to 1988, and then
in London, *International Textiles* is aimed at manufacturers.
It forecasts future trends and reports on couture shows.

HARDY AMIES

page twenty-five

Ruth Freeman, Hardy Amies suit for Harrods promotional
material, *c*.1951. Private Collection.

Hardy Amies, who had established himself in 1946, was quick
to respond to the demand for ready-to-wear clothing that
carried the cachet of a couture label and opened a boutique
at his Savile Row premises.

page twenty-six

RONALD PATERSON

Ruth Freeman, Ronald Paterson coat for Harrods promotional
material, *c*.1951. Private Collection.

Paterson was well-known for his classic designs in tweed,
of which this is a superb example.

WORTH

page twenty-four

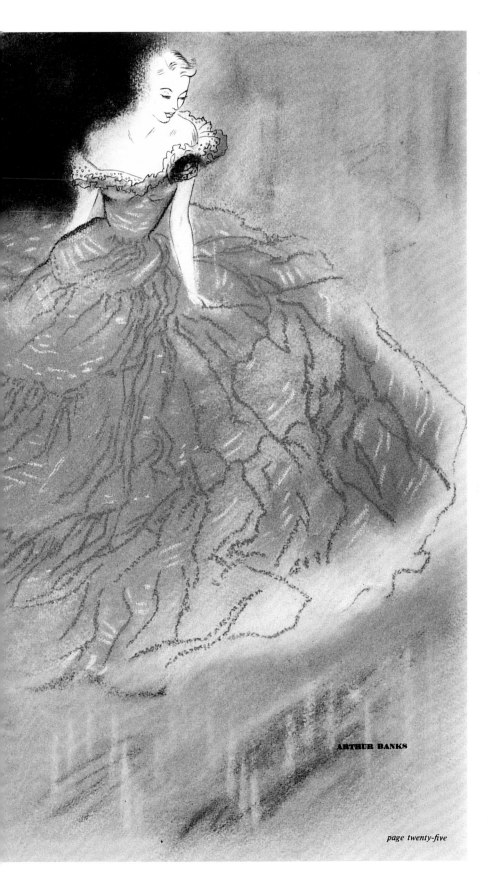

ARTHUR BANKS

page twenty-five

Ruth Freeman, Arthur Banks
evening gowns for Harrods
promotional material, *c*.1951.
Private Collection.

Frothy evening gowns are featured
in this illustration by Ruth Freeman,
a Canadian-born artist who trained
at the Slade School of Art, going on
to work for *Vogue, Good Housekeeping,
Harper's Bazaar* and *She*. She also
reported on the Paris shows for
various newspapers and worked
in advertising.

"Léocadia" d'Henry à la Pensée
en tussah "Balibali"
de Laffolay

"Kim" de Vera Boréa
Tissu "l'Emigrant"
de Suzanne Fontan

Modèles et tissus déposés, reproduction interdite.

Anonymous, Plate from *L'Officiel de la couleur des industries de la mode: Cahiers bleus*, No. 12, *c*.1952. Courtesy The Stapleton Collection.

The silhouette of Dior's New Look continued to be a strong influence on other designers. Here a pink tussah silk cocktail dress by Henry à la Pensée is paired with a gaily printed summer frock by Vera Boréa.

L'OFFICIEL DE LA COULEUR
DES INDUSTRIES DE LA MODE
CAHIERS BLEUS Nº 12

*Sous la pluie
de Lanvin Castillo
en "Pluvionyl" de
Bucol*

*"Miss Helliet" de
Lanvin Castillo
en nylon quadrille
"Benedictine" de
Bucol*

Modèles et tissus déposés, reproduction interdite

Anonymous, Plate from *L'Officiel de la couleur des industries
de la mode: Cahiers bleus*, No.12, *c.*1952. Courtesy The
Stapleton Collection.

Two raincoats by Lanvin Castillo. Jeanne Lanvin died in 1946
and in 1950 Antonio Canovas del Castillo (who had been
designing haute couture for Elizabeth Arden in New York) was
appointed chief designer. These practical raincoats are made
in nylon fabric, swatches of which are attached.

Beryl Hartland, Sketch for Horrockses advertisement, *c*.1952.
Artist's Collection.

Horrockses, a major cotton manufacturing firm, was founded
in Preston, Lancashire, in 1791. Its range of goods for household
use was extended in 1946 with the launch of Horrockses
Fashions. Its crisp, high-quality cotton dresses became a staple
garment for many women in the 1950s.

Beryl Hartland, Sketch for Horrockses advertisement, *c*.1952.
Artist's Collection.

Beryl Hartland's illustrations were featured in many newspapers
and magazines during the 1950s. Her exuberant style was well
suited to the sweeping glamour of this period.

Beryl Hartland, Advertisement for Horrockses, *The Queen*,
June 1953. Private Collection.

Horrockses commissioned well-known artists such as Eduardo
Paolozzi and Graham Sutherland to design its prints. The
company promoted the glamour of cotton and underlined quality
by sending its design team to the Paris collections and placing
advertisements in all the high-fashion magazines. Despite
their modest cost, Horrockses' dresses were worn by members
of the British royal family.

René Bouché, Advertisement for Pringle, *The Queen*,
June 1953. Private Collection.

Pringle of Scotland was founded in the early 19th century and
still produces fine cashmere knitwear today. Bouché was among
the last of the old-school illustrators. He worked for *Vogue* until
his death in 1963.

Constance Wibaut, California Chic, *Elseviers Weekblad*, 1953.
Collection of The Gemeentemuseum Den Haag.

Los Angeles casual wear, depicted in a Dutch weekly newspaper
(published since 1945), features skintight capri pants, off-the-
shoulder tops and the immaculate grooming for which American
women were renowned.

La vogue des robes imprimées associées à de très souples manteaux de soie a conduit le grand couturier Christian Dior à construire cet ensemble ravissant. La robe est en soie ornée de bouquets. Le manteau est rose vif.

Cet ensemble noir de Hubert de Givenchy oppose à une jupe étroite, une veste décolletée en rond et boutonnée devant, aux manches trois-quarts. Un bijou de strass est piqué au bas de l'une d'elles scintillant de feux vifs.

René Gruau, Dress by Dior, *L'Officiel de la couture et de la mode de Paris*, March 1953. Colour lithograph. Courtesy The Bridgeman Art Library.

A vibrant pink flowered dress in silk is worn under a supple silk coat. Dior is now referred to as 'le grand couturier'. *L'Officiel de la couture et de la mode* was launched in Paris in 1921.

René Gruau, Dress by Givenchy, *L'Officiel de la couture et de la mode de Paris*, March 1953. Colour lithograph. Courtesy The Bridgeman Art Library.

Hubert de Givenchy established his house in 1952 and became known for his understated elegance. His most famous client was Audrey Hepburn, for whom he designed many film costumes, including those for *Breakfast at Tiffany's* in 1961.

Sir Norman Hartnell, Queen Elizabeth II in coronation robes,
1953. Courtesy The Royal Collection.

During 40 years of designing for royalty (for which he was knighted
in 1977), Hartnell helped to create the iconic image necessary for
the sovereign, as can be seen in his illustration for the Queen's
coronation gown. He used his experience in the theatre to create
a garment that would work well on the television screen. The
white satin gown was richly embroidered with coloured flowers
emblematic of the four corners of the kingdom and the dominions.

René Gruau, Advertisement for Jaeger, 1954. Private Collection.

A summery dress by Jaeger, for whom Gruau did a long-running advertising campaign that helped to establish a strong brand identity.

René Gruau, Advertisement for Jaeger, 1954. Private Collection.

Jaeger has always been known for its quality garments and
use of British fabrics and knitwear. A boldly checked overcoat
epitomizes its production values.

Tailored by Simpson craftsmen
for anyone whose appearance is of
first importance, a Daks double-
breasted town suit is an asset
to its wearer. At the same time he
enjoys the comfort-in-action
of Daks trousers and the well-
balanced cut of the jacket.

Hof, Daks suit from Simpson's catalogue, 1954. Courtesy Daks/Simpson Archive.

A suave businessman in a double-breasted, checked town suit. Details of cut and construction were essential in this kind of publication and could be represented more clearly by illustration than by photography.

At Wimbledon or Lords. On the plane to Paris. At a house party. The Daks leisure suit is single-breasted with patch pockets and is tailored with the same skill that distinguishes the most formal town suit.

Hof, Daks town suit from Simpson's catalogue, 1954. Courtesy Daks/Simpson Archive.

A single-breasted leisure suit is given extra glamour by the plane in the background. International travel boomed when commercial jet airliners came into operation in the late 1950s.

Photograph of Dior's A-line suit, February 1955. Courtesy
CORBIS/Bettman. Photographer: Stéphane Tavoularis

The New Look was followed by the A-, Y- and H-lines.
Dior's A-line suppresses the bust and waist and emphasizes
the letter shape with a pleated skirt.

René Gruau, Dior's A-line suit, British *Vogue*, March 1955.
Courtesy The Condé Nast Publications Ltd.

Gruau's mastery of outline allows Dior's design to be depicted
in a few assured strokes, again demonstrating the transformative
power of illustration.

Constance Wibaut, Original illustration of Balenciaga for
Elseviers Weekblad, February 1955. Ink and gouache on paper.
Collection of The Gemeentemuseum Den Haag.

Balenciaga's disciplined styles for summer 1955. Constance
Wibaut trained as a sculptor. She illustrated for several Dutch
magazines and newspapers, notably, from 1953 to 1969, for
Elseviers Weekblad and *Elseviers Magazine*. During the early 1950s,
she also worked for *Women's Wear Daily*, the *Houston Chronicle*
and the *Daily Telegraph*, London.

Constance Wibaut, Original drawing for *Elseviers Weekblad*,
1956. Collection of The Gemeentemuseum Den Haag.

Fur-trimmed coats and elegant suits record the trend towards
a narrower silhouette. High hat styles imitate the beehive hairdo
popular in the late 1950s and early 1960s.

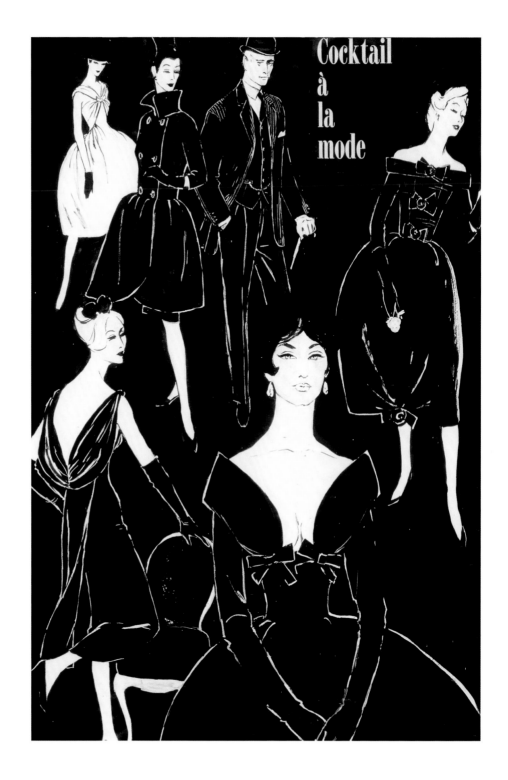

Constance Wibaut, 'Cocktail à la mode'. Original drawing for *Elseviers Weekblad*, 1957. Collection of The Gemeentemuseum Den Haag.

The cocktail dress, a postwar innovation, bridged the gap between daywear and formal eveningwear. It was short, but still worn with formal elbow-length gloves.

Alfredo Bouret, Estrava separates, British *Vogue*, January 1957.
Courtesy The Condé Nast Publications Ltd.

More youthful styles begin to emerge in the late 1950s: 'a new
young way to look in the cold...T-shirt tights are an American
idea.' Matching tights and tops are contrasted with button-through
skirts, one in sapphire mohair and one in purple felt.

Alfredo Bouret, Jacqmar separates, British *Vogue*, July 1957.
Courtesy The Condé Nast Publications Ltd.

'Brilliant velvet at-home pants, coolie length, and a whirling
chrysanthemum-print silk shirt in one of Jacqmar's famous
scarf designs.'

Anonymous, Advertisement for Kayser Bondor, *c*.1957.
Courtesy Museum of Costume, Bath.

In this advertisement, Kayser Bondor, an Anglo-American lingerie
and hosiery manufacturer, appeals to the younger woman.
Nylon, synthesized by Du Pont in 1938, revolutionized postwar
underwear and hosiery.

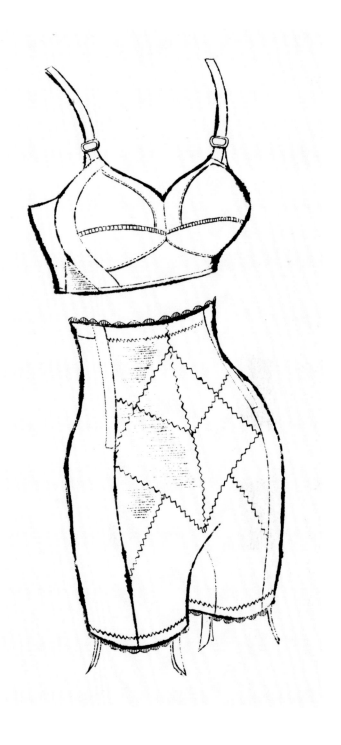

Andy Warhol, Bra and girdle, *c.*1958. Ink on Strathmore paper. Courtesy CORBIS.

An early fashion illustration by Andy Warhol, demonstrating the importance of detail in lingerie advertisements. Despite the absence of a figure, the currently fashionable silhouette is indicated by the cone-shaped breasts of the bra and the stomach-flattening panty girdle.

Andy Warhol, Woman and car, *c*.1959.
Ink and Dr Martin's aniline dye on Strathmore paper.
Courtesy CORBIS.

Since the early 1900s, the car had been used in fashion
illustration as a symbol of modernity – here Warhol gives
it as much importance as the figure.

Andy Warhol, Woman with flowers and plants, *c*.1960.
Courtesy CORBIS.

The stark simplicity of the garments is enlivened
by Warhol's use of rainbow stripes overlaying the figure,
a new idiom in illustration.

Hof, Advertisement for Simpson's, 1959. Courtesy
Daks / Simpson Archive.

Highlighting the difference in imagery used by the 'old school'
of illustrator and Warhol's innovative work, Hof depicts
comfortable middle-class casual wear. Illustration for advertising
usually lagged behind that used in editorial.

Andy Warhol, Man in Black, *c.*1960. Ink on board.
Courtesy CORBIS.

A sharply cut Italian-style suit worn with pointed shoes
and a narrow-brimmed hat is the image of early
1960s cool.

Junichi Nakahara, Man in Black, 1961. Private Collection.

A Japanese version of 1960s cool by Junichi Nakahara, an illustrator who was a sensation in his own country in the 1950s and 1960s, combining traditional and Western aesthetic in his fashion work.

Junichi Nakahara, Girl and photomontage, *c*.1960.
Private Collection.

Western-style comic strips and cartoons had long been popular
in Japan, where they were fused with *ukiyo-e* woodblock prints
into what is now known generically as *manga*. Nakahara
references *manga* in the comic-strip-style collaged background,
as well as in the girl's large eyes, and small nose and mouth.

BERKERTEX MAKES YOU MORE BEAUTIFUL

Bobby Hillson, Advertisement for Berkertex, *c.*1960.
Artist's Collection.

Founded in 1936, Berkertex became a major British clothes
manufacturer. In 1948 its factory in Plymouth became the
largest single dressmaking unit in the world, covering nearly
ten acres. Selling mid-priced clothes for the 25-upwards
age group, its retail outlets numbered over 2,000 across
the country by the early 1970s.

Bobby Hillson, Advertisement for Berkertex, *c.*1960.
Artist's Collection.

Flat panels of pattern applied with Letratone give the image
a graphic textural interest.

Angela Landels, Sîan Phillips in Chanel Suit, *c.*1961.
Pencil on paper. Courtesy Museum of Costume, Bath.

A cardigan suit by Chanel and her signature two-tone court shoes
complement the elegance of the sitter in Landels' drawing.

Victor, Advertisement for Dolcis shoes, 1961.
Courtesy The Advertising Archives.

The stiletto heel, whose invention is usually attributed to Italian
shoe designer Salvatore Ferragamo, was widely worn in the
1950s and early 1960s.

Anonymous, Advertisement for Brevitt shoes, early 1960s.
Courtesy The Advertising Archives.

This advertisement stresses the 'Continental' appeal
of Brevitt shoes.

片足が前に出れば，巻
きつけた裾が引っ張ら
れる．引っ張られた足
の細さがそれ以上に細
くなる瞬間である．

髷という日本髪の大きさは，顔を小
さく感じさせるテクニックなのだろ
う．日本髪でなくても，このように
結い上げれば同じわけだ．背のおた
いこの塊が女性のもつ曲線にぴった
り融け合ってしまう．

97

Setsu Nagasawa, Two women in kimonos, *c*.1960.
Private Collection.

Despite depicting traditional kimonos and using traditional
media, Setsu Nagasawa, a Japanese illustrator popular
in the 1960s and 1970s, gives an interpretation that
is utterly contemporary.

上等な柔かい布は女に纏わりつく．そして束縛する．そこに女のしなやかさが生まれるらしい．

流行にとらわれず，いつでも着られるイヴニングドレス．ペンダントやチョーカーなどのアクセサリーで変化を楽しむ．

Setsu Nagasawa, Two Japanese women in Western dress, *c.*1960. Private Collection.

Nagasawa fuses the oriental aesthetic with Western fashion.

Sun and swim ideas for 1963 specially designed in Paris for "international textiles"

Idées pour le bain et la plage en 1963, conçues
à Paris pour "international textiles"

· Poncho of navy and black terry cloth. Thick
  white rope belt.
· Poncho en tissu éponge bleu marine et noir.
  Large cordelière blanche.
· Poncho aus marineblauem und weissem
  Frottierstoff mit dicker, weisser Schnur als
  Gürtel.

· Beach tunic of white terry cloth, worn over
  slim black jersey pants.
· Tunique de plage en tissu éponge blanc sur
  un étroit pantalon en jersey noir.
· Strand-Tunika aus weissem Frottierstoff über
  enger, schwarzer Jersey-Hose.

54 international textiles

Hervé Dubly, 'Sun and Swim Ideas', *International Textiles*, 1962.
Private Collection.

Radically new silhouettes hint at the innovation of early sixties
fashion. Dubly worked mainly for French *Vogue*.

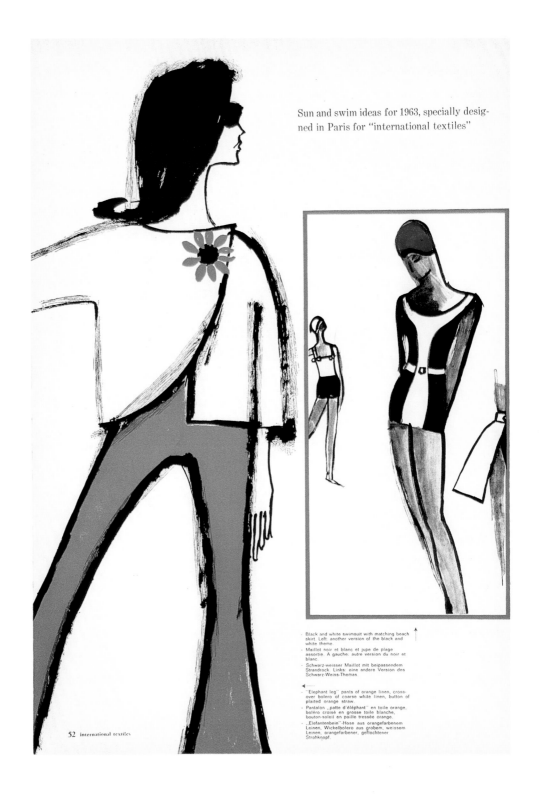

Sun and swim ideas for 1963, specially designed in Paris for "international textiles"

- Black and white swimsuit with matching beach
  skirt. Left: another version of the black and
  white theme.
- Maillot noir et blanc et jupe de plage
  assortie. A gauche: autre version du noir et
  blanc.
- Schwarz-weisser Maillot mit beipassendem
  Strandrock. Links: eine andere Version des
  Schwarz-Weiss-Themas.

- "Elephant leg" pants of orange linen, cross-
  over bolero of coarse white linen, button of
  plaited orange straw.
- Pantalon „patte d'éléphant" en toile orange,
  boléro croisé en grosse toile blanche,
  bouton-soleil en paille tressée orange.
- „Elefantenbein"-Hose aus orangefarbenem
  Leinen, Wickelbolero aus grobem, weissem
  Leinen, orangefarbener, geflochtener
  Strohknopf.

52 international textiles

Hervé Dubly, 'Sun and Swim Ideas', *International Textiles*, 1962.
Private Collection.

On the left, 'elephant pants' anticipate the flared trousers
of the later sixties. Towelling fabric or 'terry cloth' for beachwear
became popular at this time.

René Gruau, Original illustration for cover of *Sir*, early 1960s.
Brush drawing, ink and watercolour. Courtesy Galerie Bartsch
& Chariau, Munich.

In a two-dimensional image, Gruau uses Op Art motifs and flat
colour in a radically innovative illustration. Published by the
International Textiles group, *Sir* was a quarterly magazine
for the trade, reporting the latest trends in menswear.

René Gruau, Original illustration for cover of *International Textiles*, May 1962. Brush drawing, ink and watercolour. Courtesy Galerie Bartsch & Chariau, Munich.

Almost hidden by the beach towel, the figure imparts the air of mystery which Gruau often used in his work.

BLAZER JACKETS

Vestes blazer

Blazer-Moden

44 • SIR

René Gruau, Blazer jackets, *Sir*, 1963. Private Collection.

The 'peacock revolution' in the 1960s brought in coloured suits,
flowered shirts and a more relaxed attitude to men's fashion,
here still influenced by sharp Italian tailoring.

Gruau, with his new blazer jackets, reflects the feeling for casual elegance on semi-formal occasions. The blazer returns with traditional patch pockets and brass buttons but with narrow revers and wide, natural shoulders

Gruau introduit dans ses nouveaux blazers une élégance sportive qui convient bien pour les petites occasions. On y retrouve les traditionnelles poches plaquées et boutons dorés, mais les revers sont étroits et les épaules, naturelles et larges

Gruau bringt mit seinen neuen Blazern eine sportliche Eleganz für zwanglose Gelegenheiten. Wiederkehr der traditionellen aufgesetzten Taschen und Messingknöpfe, jedoch schmale Revers und breite, natürliche Schulterlinie

SIR • 45

René Gruau, Blazer jackets, *Sir*, 1963. Private Collection.

Gruau is credited with designing these blazer jackets. So closely attuned to fashion, illustrators have often been required to set a mood, indicate a trend or indeed, actually design garments.

Tod Draz, 'Les Idées "Choc"', *International Textiles*, 1963/4.
Private Collection.

The accompanying article is entitled 'Fashion at Turning Point'
and goes on to highlight the divergence between the traditional
'clientele' collections and those which 'express a free and
easy style' by designers who want to 'free themselves from
the influence of Balenciaga'.

i.t.- 83

Tod Draz, Patou, Courrèges, Dior and Capucci, *International Textiles*, 1963/4. Private Collection.

The boxy, geometric silhouettes are elongated by tall-crowned hats. Roberto Capucci established himself in Italian couture, or *alta moda*, in the early 1950s. The House of Patou is perhaps best known today for its perfume, Joy, launched in 1935 and still a bestseller despite its high cost.

Balenciaga

Constance Wibaut, '64

Constance Wibaut, Suit by Balenciaga, 1964. Artist's Collection.

Known as the 'designer's designer', Balenciaga was a master
cutter. His loose, hip-length suit jacket exemplifies his exploration
of a new, sculptural silhouette, and his influence can clearly
be seen in the work of his protégé Courrèges (see opposite).

Anonymous, Trouser suit by André Courrèges, 1964. Courtesy
Museum of Costume, Bath.

Courrèges' seminal 1964 Space Age collection helped
to popularize trouser suits. The accessories – 'space helmet'
hat, white gloves and pointed white boots – were all elements
of his signature look.

Bobby Hillson, Original illustration of the Paris collections for *The Observer*, *c*.1965. Pencil on paper. Artist's Collection.

Hemlines are beginning to rise. By its nature, the miniskirt was suited to younger women. For many older women, the final acceptance of trousers into the fashionable wardrobe in the mid-1960s came as a relief.

Bobby Hillson, Original illustration of the Paris collections
for *The Observer*, *c.*1965. Pencil on paper. Artist's Collection.

Bobby Hillson illustrated for numerous top magazines and
periodicals during the 1960s. She set up the Fashion MA course
at Central Saint Martins, London, and ran it from 1978 to 1995.

Wool crêpe suit with bead-
bound neck from Deliss.
James Wedge crochet
cloche and enamel brooch
from Top Gear.

Caroline Smith, Deliss suit and accessories, *The Queen*,
June 1965. Artist's Collection.

Informed by Pop Art, flat, bright colours are used to depict two
of the most iconic features of the 1960s – the Union Jack, symbol
of 'Swinging London', and the miniskirted 'dolly bird', her face
painted with hearts that anticipate the hippy style.

Knitted dress, with cutaway
armholes, checkerboard beret by
James Wedge, kid lace-up shoes
with see-through toes by Moya.
All from Top Gear.

Caroline Smith, Crochet minidress, *The Queen*, June 1965.
Artist's Collection.

Relaunched in 1957 by Jocelyn Stevens, *The Queen* magazine
provided a punchy, uncompromising mix of fashion, thought-
provoking articles and society gossip within a glossy new format.
This issue included a map of trendy boutiques where 'you can
expect a touch of madness or a zany inspiration'.

Paul Christadoulou, Evening ensemble by Clive, Lanctan catalogue, Autumn 1965. CSM Archive.

Lanctan, a leather-tanning company based in Lancashire, featured leading designers' work in their catalogue, alongside leather samples and colour swatches for shoes and handbags. Clive's brocade evening jacket is worn over a bare-shouldered sheath.

Bill Baker, Dress by Caroline Charles, Lanctan catalogue, Spring 1966. CSM Archive.

A little black dress from Caroline Charles with 'Quaker collar and cuffs' is contrasted with Art-Nouveau-style motifs.

Ossie Clark, Designs for Maxwell Fabrics, 1965/6. Courtesy
V&A Images.

Early designs by Ossie Clark, inspired by monochrome Op Art
motifs. After graduating from the Royal College of Art in 1964,
Clark became the designer of choice to the London pop scene.

Sylvia Ayton, Design sketches for the Fulham Road Clothes
Shop, *c*.1968. Artist's Collection.

The Fulham Road Clothes Shop was owned jointly by Zandra
Rhodes and Sylvia Ayton, both recent graduates of the Royal
College of Art. The designs show high collars, less severe
hairstyles and an increasing emphasis on the shoulders.

Constance Wibaut, Sketches from Paris, 1966. Collection of The Gemeentemuseum Den Haag.

Wibaut's sketches show the clean, spare lines, imaginative cutting and helmet-style hats associated with Pierre Cardin.

Constance Wibaut, Sketch from Paris, *c.*1966. Collection
of The Gemeentemuseum Den Haag.

Cardin's menswear was truly innovative – here a zipped gilet
is worn over a black roll-neck. Tight trousers and a helmet
hat complete the outfit. Cardin was one of the first designers
to promote unisex styles, a growing feature of late
20th-century fashion.

René Gruau, Original illustration for cover of *International Textiles*,1967. Brush drawing, ink and gouache. Courtesy Galerie Bartsch & Chariau, Munich.

Gruau sets his illustration against contemporary lettering. Graphic design was influenced by the sixties psychedelic culture.

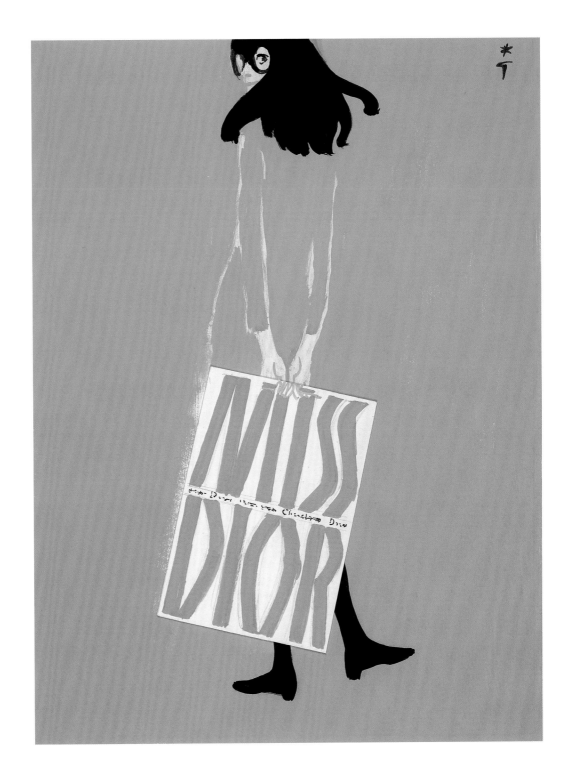

René Gruau, Original illustration for advertisement for Dior perfume, 1967/8. Brush drawing, gouache and collage. Courtesy Galerie Bartsch & Chariau, Munich.

Gruau's campaign for Dior perfumes continued into the 1980s and was an ongoing contribution to illustration through a lean period for the genre.

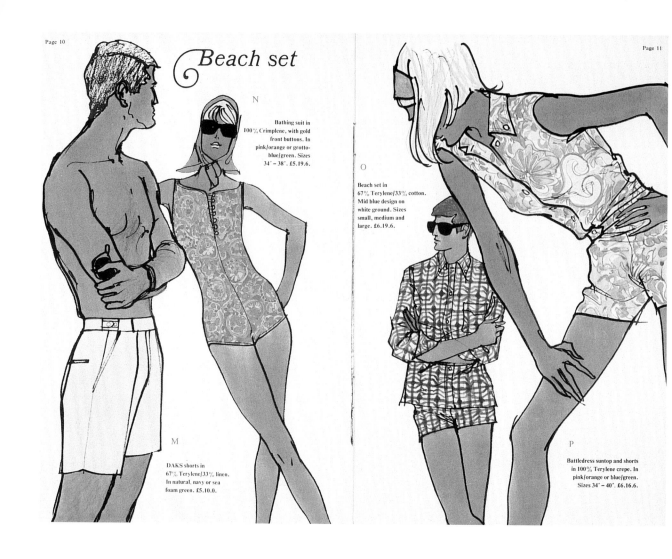

Beach set

N

Bathing suit in
100% Crimplene, with gold
front buttons. In
pink/orange or grotto-
blue/green. Sizes
34″ – 38″. £5.19.6.

O

Beach set in
67% Terylene/33% cotton.
Mid blue design on
white ground. Sizes
small, medium and
large. £6.19.6.

M

DAKS shorts in
67% Terylene/33% linen.
In natural, navy or sea
foam green. £5.10.0.

P

Battledress suntop and shorts
in 100% Terylene crepe. In
pink/orange or blue/green.
Sizes 34″ – 40″. £6.16.6.

Eric Stemp, 'Beach Set', Simpson's catalogue, *c*.1967. Courtesy
Daks/Simpson's archive.

New fabrics for swimwear include Crimplene and Terylene. Eric
Stemp's precise drawings were a feature of many magazines after
the war, and from 1964 he became official advertising illustrator
for Simpson's of Piccadilly.

Her nylon anorak - complete with hood
in shocking pink. Also in navy. Sizes
10-14. £12.10.0.
His reversible nylon anorak has a novel spring
release ticket holder. In light blue with black
trim or red with black. Both reverse to plain
black. £12.10.0. Worn with DAKS two-way
stretch, worsted/lycra ski trousers. Black
or navy. £18.0.0.

She sports a Stoffel Terylene/
cotton anorak in amber,
light blue, or geranium.
Very simple, very practical.
Sizes 10-18. £12.15.0.
Worn with ski trousers in
worsted/nylon in black,
navy or pink. £10.10.0.

He wears a royal blue nylon
anorak. Also in black or
bottle green. £10.10.0.
Worn with worsted and lycra
ski trousers, in navy or
black. £11.0.0.

Eric Stemp, Two illustrations of
skiwear, Simpson's catalogue, *c.*1967.
Courtesy Daks/Simpson's Archive.

Developed by DuPont before the
Second World War, nylon was reserved
for hosiery and underwear until its
suitability for activity clothing was
exploited in the 1960s.

Antonio Lopez, Original illustration of Victor Joris for 'Fashion of the Times', *New York Times Magazine*, 1965. Pentel, collage and black overlay film. Courtesy Galerie Bartsch & Chariau, Munich.

An early work by Antonio inspired by Pop artist Roy Lichtenstein. Antonio's chameleon-like ability to adapt to the contemporary art scene enabled him to reinvent his style throughout his career.

Antonio Lopez, Original illustration of summer sportswear
for British *Vogue*, April 1968. Pentel and colour overlay film on
paper. Courtesy Galerie Bartsch & Chariau, Munich.

Nylon quilted and zipped all-in-one suits for water-skiing by
Colsenet at Simpson's, modelled by Donna Mitchell. The swirling
print, long Art-Nouveau-style hair and tinted sunglasses reflect
the arrival of the psychedelic age.

E. Bernais, Miniskirts and tops by Gina Fratini, 1968.
Courtesy Museum of Costume, Bath.

The miniskirt, worn here with a variety of tops, was at its shortest
around 1967. The childlike models express the 'baby-doll' look
associated with the decade, underlined by huge round eyes
emphasized by even rounder sunglasses.

The culotte cult in Tricel

at

ⁿeatawear

Two-way, new-way, all-shaped culottes.
Bright for day-time, play-time or party-time.
And all in Tricel, so easy-care is second nature.
Culottes at Neatawear. They're *strides* ahead!

From a large selection of
Neatawear fashions in

TRICEL

Left: Evening culottes in oranges or
purples. Sizes 10-14. About 8½gns.
Centre: Shirtwaister culottes,
yellow/green, pink/yellow, blue/
mauve. Sizes 10-14. About 99/11.
Right: Play culottes, pink/green, blue/
mauve, yellow/purple. Sizes 10-14. About 89/11.

Available at most Neatawear Branches
or through Postal Service at:—
12-14 Clipstone Street, London, W.1.

Bobby Hillson, Advertisement for Tricel, *c.*1968.
Artist's Collection.

Culotte jumpsuits in Tricel, another synthetic fibre that was used
to make fun, easy-to-wear, inexpensive clothes.

Corduroy
Trench Coat
and skirt

T Shirt dress
and college scarf

Polo dress
and jerkin

Hacking jacket set

Cotton jersey
cardigan set

Negligee and nightie

Pirate set

Anonymous, Barbara Hulanicki, from Biba catalogue, 1968/9.
Private Collection.

The Biba mail-order catalogue enabled provincial customers
to buy the look. In 1973 Hulanicki took over the former Derry
& Toms department store in London, building on its attractions
as an Art Deco emporium. It closed two years later after
running into financial difficulties.

A   B   C

D   E   F   G

All colours and prints in the catalogue have been dyed specially for Biba. The two granny prints are recut from original 1910 fabric designs.

Short printed dress by Dorville in Courtelle single jersey. Fully lined. Style 207. About £22.4.

Short check dress and scarf by Dorville in Courtelle and wool woven. Fully lined. Style 212. About £21.4.

Arrive barely armed

Long printed dress by Dorville in Courtelle twill. Fully lined. Style 208. About £23.16. Also short version. About £18.

Three sure ways to emerge victorious from any social encounters. One in ravishing, lushly printed Courtelle Twill; one in Courtelle and wool woven; one in supple Courtelle jersey. All bearing the exclusive Dorville label.

Colours are out to kill at sight.

Now choose whether you're better armed with bare knees too.

IN COURTELLE

Anonymous, Advertisement for Dorville designs in Courtelle fabrics, 1969. Private Collection.

Dorville, established soon after the First World War, specialized in casual, but elegant, clothes. The company was one of the first in Britain to apply US sizing and production methods and later collaborated to launch Courtelle with a major promotional and advertising campaign.

Dress and jacket knitted in Courtelle
by Louis Feraud at Rembrandt.
Style 9115. About £24.

Dress knitted in Courtelle
by Louis Feraud
at Rembrandt.
Style 9122. About £25.

Anonymous, Advertisement for Louis Feraud designs in Courtelle
fabrics, 1969. Private Collection.

Many designers in the 1960s explored the potential of synthetic
fibres, adding to their cachet. Louis Feraud, famous for his use of
colour in clothes, opened his ready-to-wear salon in Paris in 1955.

Celia Birtwell, Fabric designs and illustrations, 1969/70.
Courtesy V&A Images.

By the late 1960s, the hippy style was replacing the hard-edged
designs and stiffer fabrics of previous years. A new aesthetic
of swirling pattern and colour lent itself to floaty, sheer fabrics,
such as those used by Celia Birtwell (Ossie Clark's wife)
and Zandra Rhodes.

Sunset
through a
pr

BODY
BLOUSE

Robert Passantino, 'Body Blouse'. Original illustration for
Women's Wear Daily, 1970. Marker and collage. Artist's Collection.

New concepts in soft, unsupportive underwear were
prompted by the development of synthetic fabrics.
Robert Passantino, a staff illustrator on *WWD* for over
20 years, introduced a clean, minimal style that lent itself
to reproducing well on newsprint.

Robert Passantino, 'Free Form'. Original illustration for
Women's Wear Daily, 1970. Rapidograph, prismacolour pencil
and collage. Artist's Collection.

Tights were essential with miniskirts, hotpants and jumpsuits.
They were available in a multitude of patterns and colours from
the mid- to late 1960s.

Antonio Lopez, 'Back to Nature'. Original drawing for British *Vogue*, July 1970. Pentel and overlay film. Courtesy Galerie Bartsch & Chariau, Munich.

An embroidered linen shepherd's smock and matching trousers embody the trend towards rediscovery of a utopian past and the popularity of authentic handicrafts.

Antonio Lopez, 'St. Tropez'. Original drawing for French *Vogue*, 1970. Pentel, collage and overlay film. Courtesy Galerie Bartsch & Chariau, Munich.

Antonio's dense fusion of Pop Art, comic strip and psychedelic motifs still manages to show the detail of the clothes, modelled by Donna Jordan.

18. Her raincoat is in
50% cotton, 50% Dacron.
Beige or brown,
both with brown Borg lining.
Sizes 10-16. £30.00.

24. Eyecatching suede trench coat in montana or brick. Sizes 12–18. £67.00.

25. Luxurious leather jacket. Dark antique brown. £49.00.

Simpson
PICCADILLY

Eric Stemp (left and above), Raincoats and tweeds for Simpson's catalogue, *c*.1971. Courtesy Daks/Simpson's Archive.

Mainstream fashion for the more conventional customer continues to promote classic British style and fabrics. Stemp taught Fashion Drawing at Central Saint Martins and the 'attenuated elegance' typical of the college style can be seen in his work.

TUTAMBAN EM
Blue Coney with
RACOON Collar
£280
Antonio 72

Antonio Lopez, 'Fur for Glamour'. Original illustration for British *Vogue*, October 1972. Charcoal and pencil on paper. Courtesy Galerie Bartsch & Chariau, Munich.

1940s glamour in relatively inexpensive dyed furs. Animal skins and fake furs were popular until the anti-fur campaigns of the late 1980s. Modelled by Grace Coddington, then British *Vogue*'s iconic fashion editor.

Antonio Lopez, 'Capezio'. Original illustration, *c*.1972. Charcoal and pencil on paper. Courtesy Galerie Bartsch & Chariau, Munich.

Capezio of New York started in 1887 as a maker of ballet footwear. Their long-sole ballet shoe was featured by Claire McCardell in her 1941 collection, thereafter ensuring that dance and exercise wear, lines the company would later venture into, would enter the fashion arena.

Caroline Smith, Illustration for *Destiny*, *c*.1970.
Artist's Collection.

A combination of glamour and nostalgia characterizes
late 1960s/early 1970s high-street clothes.

Caroline Smith, Illustration for *Destiny*, *c*.1970.
Artist's Collection.

Caroline Smith illustrated for many magazines during
the 1960s and 1970s, including *Vogue*.

Caroline Smith, Advertisement for C&A, *c*.1973.
Artist's Collection.

Smith depicts the tactile qualities of fake fur. C&A,
a Dutch-owned store, continues as a purveyor
of inexpensive fashions on the high street in Europe.

Caroline Smith, Advertisement for C&A, *c*.1973.
Artist's Collection.

Smith often set multiple images within a frame. Here
she depicts the peasant-style prints that were a feature
of the ethnic influences popular at this time.

'We were a generation of British youth who had lived our entire lives in the glow of pop culture, and had been through every teenage sartorial twist from the twist onward. We were innately versed in every nuance of every look and trend. … The past was a dressing-up box.'

Robert Elms, *The Way We Wore*, **2005**

The story of fashion in the latter part of the twentieth century is hard to trace. It is characterized by the breakdown of the traditional couture industry; by the immediacy of the response of the world's clothes manufacturing industry to the demands of its high-street consumers; and by an emphasis on individuality which has resulted in the fragmentation of fashion into a multitude of styles. Ironically, a further effect has been a certain global sartorial homogeneity on the part of those wishing to reject the perceived excesses of the high-fashion world and to renounce the label of 'fashion victim'. However, even though denim, T-shirts and trainers are prime examples of anti-fashion, they still carry a hierarchy of exclusive designer brands.

What finally put an end to the hegemony of couture, however, was the anarchic nihilism of punk. Born in London's underground club scene of the mid-seventies, punk can be seen as the antithesis of the hippies' idealistic optimism, appearing as it did in a darker period of rising unemployment and economic stagnation. The style was inseparable from music, particularly that of the Sex Pistols, whose manager, Malcolm McLaren, was the partner of the innovative British designer Vivienne Westwood. A succession of shops in Chelsea initially revisited earlier subcultural styles such as teddy boys' and bikers' gear, then moved on to fetish wear. But by 1976, when the Sex Pistols first appeared on stage, the look was one of anarchy and outrage – sadomasochistic black bondage trousers, T-shirts with explicit slogans, mohican hairstyles, safety pins and body piercing. It was the first street movement that gave its female members equal importance in terms of dress, challenging all previous concepts of femininity with its deliberate, slovenly unattractiveness.

Vivienne Westwood continued to push the boundaries of high fashion, blending historical references and traditional techniques and fabrics with ever-evolving concepts of female identity and eroticism. The 'new romantic' look, based on the London post-punk club scene of the late seventies and early eighties, was transposed by her into couture. Westwood remains at the forefront of the dynamic contribution British fashion designers have made to the industry, a contribution that has seen many of them head up major Paris couture houses: John Galliano at Dior, Alexander McQueen at Givenchy and Stella McCartney at Chloé. All trained at British art colleges, and have made fertile use of the inspirational influences provided by London's underground scene.

In the commercialized mainstream fashion industry the economic boom of the early eighties brought with it the 'power dressing' symbolic of that decade. Referencing forties glamour, the archetypal suit with its short skirt and heavily padded shoulders combined sex and business, while the puffball 'pouf' skirt (popularized by the French designer Christian Lacroix) typified evening glamour. Power dressing was taken to its extremity when underwear became

Vivienne Westwood, Cover of *Fashion Flash*, November 1981. Courtesy V&A Images.

The text underlines the importance of street fashion in London, linking it with Vivienne Westwood's latest collection, Savage. The illustration depicts the anarchic spirit brought by British subcultural fashion into the wider arena.

Steven Stipelman, Tweed coat and separates for *Women's Wear Daily*, 1984. Artist's Collection.

Stipelman exaggerates the oversized, padded shoulders typical of 1980s 'power dressing' and highlights the textures of fabrics.

a feature of outerwear, expressing a new kind of female emancipation: an overtly sexy look that was both a challenge and a threat. The gold, pointed-bra corset by Jean-Paul Gaultier worn onstage by Madonna on her late eighties tours exemplified this look. Skintight leotards and leggings also revealed the body as the aerobics craze got under way. Garments such as these, previously worn only by dancers and sportsmen, were closely followed by the unisex tracksuit and trainers. All entered the everyday wardrobe for good, with sportswear brands such as Nike and Adidas claiming their own territory on the high street.

A counterpart to the provocative, flamboyant look of the 'yuppie' decade was the sophisticated, pared-down elegance that became the signature, from the seventies onward, of American designers such as Geoffrey Beene, Halston, Calvin Klein and Donna Karan. Luxurious fabrics and a restrained palette were used to create versatile wardrobes for career-minded women, emphasizing the status value of simplicity. This concept was also employed by the Italian designer Giorgio Armani, whose 'soft dressing' eschewed eighties excess. His virtually anonymous look is the opposite of the flashy logos and decadent appeal of his fellow-countrymen Gianni Versace, Franco Moschino, and Domenico Dolce and Stefano Gabbana of Dolce & Gabbana.

Ralph Lauren, whose Polo label was launched in 1967, developed the American preppy look, later basing his collections on a nostalgic reinterpretation of classic menswear and country clothing and on early twentieth-century cowboy style. Furnishing his outlets in the manner of an English gentleman's club or a prairie ranch-house in the Midwest, he marketed not only clothes, but also an aspirational lifestyle, providing home accessories and furnishings to match. He was part of a trend that continues today, with fashion designers branding their own ranges of homewares, from bed linen to wallpaper to china, underlining the fact that fashion is no longer just about clothes, but pervades every aspect of contemporary culture.

The influence of Japanese designers on Western fashion was felt from the seventies on. They brought a blend of their own cultural minimalism, traditional textile motifs coupled with the development of radical new textile technology, and a new intellectualism. Kenzo Takada, Kansai Yamamoto and Issey Miyake were followed in the eighties by Rei Kawakubo of Comme des Garçons and Yohji Yamamoto, both of whose fondness for black, unstructured layering exploring concepts of body image, ethnicity and gender, was highly influential. Deconstructed clothing – the antithesis of fashion as Christian Dior understood it – was promoted by a group of Antwerp designers, known as the 'Antwerp Six', including Dries van Noten, Anne Demeulemeester and Martin Margiela, whose late nineties collections expressed themes of decay and destruction, while at Givenchy Alexander McQueen often uses motifs of threat and anxiety in his glamorous yet edgy designs.

In the mid-1980s, fashion began to react against the decade's conspicuous consumption and to reflect new concerns about the environment and globalization. It entered the political arena when Katherine Hamnett famously wore her T-shirt emblazoned with the logo '58% don't want Pershing', from her 1984–85 Choose Life collection, to a reception hosted by Prime Minister Margaret Thatcher. The rainbow ragbag clothing of new age travellers and environmental protesters who revisited the hippy style of previous decades reflected an increasing awareness of, and demand for, organic materials and a moral stance against the exploitation of labour in Third World countries. By the nineties, the questioning of the cultural and political status quo could be found in grunge, a look based on thrift-store chic, while the transgressive appeal of 'heroin chic' was portrayed in magazines by photographers such as Corinne Day.

During the second half of the twentieth century, fashion illustration struggled to survive, until, in the eighties, it underwent a renaissance. A new generation of artists was given an outlet in magazines such as *La Mode en peinture* (1982), Condé Nast's *Vanity* (1981) and, more recently, *Visionaire* (1991). Some of the credit for illustration's revival must also go to advertising campaigns, notably that launched by Barneys in New York, which showcased Jean-Philippe Delhomme's softly humorous paintings captioned with witty text.

Despite the lack of illustration as a dedicated element of the fashion curriculum at art colleges – notable exceptions being Parsons School and the FIT in New York, Central Saint Martins College of Art and Design (formerly St Martin's School of Art), London, and the London College of Fashion – many students now choose illustration as a career, including those who approach it from a graphics rather than a fashion training. St Martin's, the alma mater of so many currently successful designers, has prioritized drawing since its fashion course was first founded in 1931 by Muriel Pemberton, herself a gifted artist. Placing emphasis on the importance of drawing from life and under the inspirational eye of tutors such as Elizabeth Suter, Colin Barnes and Howard Tangye, the college has consistently produced fashion illustrators of note, including Gladys Perint Palmer, Jo Brocklehurst, Claire Smalley, Shari Peacock, Jason Brooks and Julie Verhoeven. Brooks pioneered the use of computer-generated fashion illustration while Verhoeven has explored the possibilities offered by interactive computer-generated images. With influential publications such as *Wallpaper*, 'lifestyle' illustration has come to the fore, encompassing all elements of fashionable living, now inseparable from fashion itself.

The versatility, accessiblity and, above all, familiarity of computer images in this age of visual overload have enabled a new relationship between viewer and the drawn image, locating them as intermediaries between photography and art, while many artists have dissolved

Ruben Alterio, Armani for *Mirabella*, III, 1997. Crayon and watercolour. Courtesy Galerie Bartsch & Chariau, Munich.

Giorgio Armani's 'soft dressing' is echoed in the delicate treatment of Alterio's illustration.

the boundaries between what might be called 'fine art' illustration, photography and computer graphics, combining all these elements successfully in their work. While the computer graphic has come to dominate alongside photography all aspects of visual media, it is perhaps ironic that a period that has seen the emergence of tools such as Adobe Photoshop and Illustrator has also witnessed a revitalization of traditional art-based forms of fashion illustration.

'Traditional' handworked illustration has continued to enjoy a revival at the turn of the millennium, with fashion illustrators often looking back to the masters of the past for stylistic inspiration. René Gruau continued to draw with vigour and dynamism until his death in 2004. His has been an ongoing influence, acknowledged by artists such as David Downton, whose own supremely elegant and always informative work sometimes echoes that of the stars of the interwar years, Eric and René Bouët-Willaumez. François Berthoud, whose career began in the early eighties, uses laborious linocut, enamel drip and folded paper cut-out techniques in his work; *Visionaire*, an exclusive limited-edition album that combines art, illustration and photography and is reminiscent in spirit of those produced in the early twentieth century, has devoted a whole issue to his work. Michael Roberts, since 1997 fashion director of *The New Yorker* and an influential stylist and photographer, uses the time-consuming technique of collage – a myriad tiny paper mosaics – to construct his witty images. He views his use of this laborious technique as a compliment to the intricate work of the designer whose garment he is depicting. Mats Gustafson also employs conventional techniques, lending his watercolours and pastels a hazy, dreamlike quality, while many 'fine artists' (if such a category still exists) have been commissioned by designers and magazines to illustrate fashion. David Remfry's 2003 advertising campaign for Stella McCartney and Grayson Perry's spread on the 2005 Paris couture shows for *Spoon* magazine exemplify this trend.

Despite all expectations, fashion illustration that is grounded in artistic practice employing time-honoured methods has managed to survive alongside that mediated by more modern processes. The representation of fashion during the last half of the twentieth century has relied heavily on photography, which has increasingly prioritized image over content. Fashion editorial spreads in which the input of stylist and photographer take precedence over the clothes, and which are frequently loaded with imagery that reflects concepts of glamour and celebrity, or the postmodern obsession with feelings of alienation, unease and introspection, seldom show clothes in any detail. The art of reading a drawn graphic image, in whatever medium it is executed, demands more from the viewer, yet represents the very function that illustration of this type should perform. As one illustrator has put it, the job of the fashion artist is to 'tell the story of the dress'.

Jason Brooks, Puscha flyer, 1996. Pen, ink and Adobe Photoshop. Artist's Collection.

This flyer, for a popular London club, is a line drawing digitally manipulated to produce flat panels of colour.

or go all out for a hole-in-one.

Dacron/cotton **DAKS** shorts (S) in pale blue
£5.0.0. (5/–). Navy lisle cotton shirt (T) sizes 38–46.
£3.9.6. (5/–). Rubber soled lightweight unlined
tie shoe (U). £6.5.0. (5/–).

Packing and delivery charges are shown in brackets.

Simpson
ICCADILLY

Eric Stemp (attr.), Advertisement for Simpson's, *c.*1975.
Courtesy Daks/Simpson's Archive.

Smart sportswear for the golf course, utilizing both synthetic
and natural fabrics. Stemp drew men equally as well as women.

36. Fine quality batiste cotton shirt, block-striped in gold, navy, ultra pink, pale blue or lilac. £4.15.0.
37. Moiré silk tie. Colour toned for each shirt. £2.15.0.
38. Sand coloured suede shoe, trimmed with metal. Micro-cellular soles. £7.10.0.

39. Simpson shirt in 100% superfine poplin. Bristol blue or melon. £4.15.0.
40. New larger shape silk tie. Black/red, navy/red, navy/sky. £3.5.0. **41.** Stretch belt in black kangaroo leather. £3.15.0.
42. Black patent shoe with metal chain. £8.10.0.

BI   Simpson (Piccadilly) Ltd London W1A 2AS 01-734 2002

Eric Stemp (attr.), Advertisement for Simpson's, *c.*1975.
Courtesy Daks / Simpson's Archive.

The 'peacock revolution' was well under way by now. Although
the clothes illustrated here are fairly conventional, they show
the acceptance of coloured shirts and patterned ties for smart
casual wear.

Elizabeth Suter, Paris collections, 1978. Ink and marker.
Artist's Collection.

Elizabeth Suter was a freelance illustrator who covered the
Paris collections four times a year and illustrated for numerous
newspapers and magazines. She also taught at Central Saint
Martins, London. Having received a formal art training, she
always emphasized to her students the importance of drawing
from a life model, clothed or unclothed.

Elizabeth Suter, Paris collections, 1978. Ink and marker.
Artist's Collection.

As drawing was forbidden at the shows, Suter developed
an extraordinary ability to remember detail and record it later.

Elizabeth Suter, Fashion Forecast, 1979. Mixed media.
Artist's Collection.

Fabric trends and colours interpreted in Suter's customary
dynamic style forecast winter fashion.

Eric Stemp, Clothes by Simpson's, Autumn 1978. Courtesy Museum of Costume, Bath.

Pleated or cut on the bias, fuller skirts with lower hemlines are worn with blouson jackets.

Beryl Hartland, Illustration for the *Daily Telegraph*, mid-late 1970s. Artist's Collection.

Hartland had a long career as a fashion illustrator, mostly with the *Telegraph* newspaper group.

Steven Stipelman, Original illustration for *Women's Wear Daily*,
1978. Artist's Collection.

Stipelman, who worked at *WWD* for many years, was one of the
illustrators given a byline, endorsing them as artists. Required
not only to record actual garments, but also to interpret the mood
of a moment, he explores here 'the seduction of a black dress',
a fashion classic since Chanel's 'little black dress' of 1926.

Colin Barnes, Pirelli Calendar Girl, late 1970s. Mixed media.
Private Collection.

Colin Barnes illustrated for many top magazines, including *Vogue*,
Elle, *Cosmopolitan* and *GAP*, until his untimely death in 1994. Like
many Central Saint Martins' graduates, he returned there
to teach.

Colin Barnes, Izzy in Bruce Oldfield, 1980. Pencil and watercolour. CSM Archive.

Oldfield specializes in intricately cut glamorous dressing for the stars. Colin Barnes' forceful style always imbues his subjects with energy and dynamism.

Antonio Lopez, Original drawing for the Russia campaign for
Bloomingdale's and the *New York Times*, 1980. Pencil on paper.
Courtesy Galerie Bartsch & Chariau, Munich.

Utilizing a different style from his other work, Antonio packs his
pencil drawing full of intense detail. Cossack costume has been
an inspiration for a number of designers. In the 1970s Saint
Laurent, for example, launched a collection based on Russian
dress, as well as others that drew from Spanish, Moroccan,
Chinese and gypsy dress. In addition to his Mondrian collection,
he has also paid homage to Picasso, Braque and Cocteau,
among others.

Antonio Lopez, 'Beauty'. Original illustration for American *Vogue*, 1980. Pencil, gouache and colour overlay film on paper. Courtesy Galerie Bartsch & Chariau, Munich.

Modelled by Leslie Lopez, now a well-known makeup artist, Antonio's illustration reflects the androgynous look typified by pop star Marilyn.

Pater Sato, Drawing, *c.*1980. Private Collection.

Sato, a graduate of the Sensu Mode Seminar in Japan, was
a successful Japanese illustrator in the 1980s and 1990s.
In 1985 he coordinated *Fashion Illustration in New York*. Here,
a Westernized model wears a fitted suit with a low decolletage
filled with roses.

Pater Sato, Drawing, *c.*1980. Private Collection.

In an unusual image, Sato combines traditional Japanese dress
with a short, modern hairstyle.

Steven Stipelman, Cover for New York Collections issue
of *Women's Wear Daily*, 1981. Artist's Collection.

Stipelman contrasts 'luxe' eveningwear with sporty day
looks. The narrow silhouette of the skirt is balanced
by widening shoulders.

René Gruau, Yves Saint Laurent, Original drawing for French
Vogue, September 1981. Gouache. Courtesy The Zahm Collection,
Germany.

The 'pouf' dress epitomized extravagant 1980s eveningwear.
Gruau uses light and shade to great effect, demonstrating that
in his seventies he is still a master of impact.

Jo Brocklehurst, Min and Val, 1982. Mixed media.
Artist's Collection.

Jo Brocklehurst, who has been called 'the unofficial chronicler
of club culture', found a rich source of models in the clubs
she frequented. Provocative slogans, ripped clothing
and dyed hair epitomize the 'in your face' look of the punk
movement in her powerful drawing.

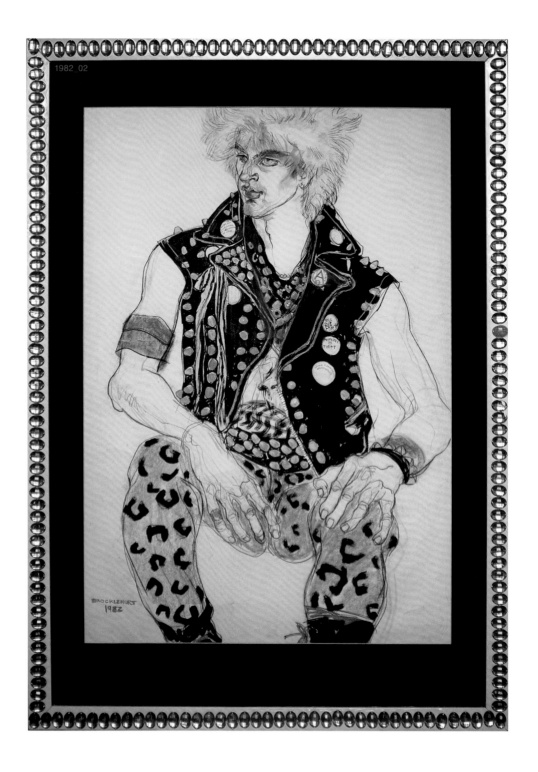

Jo Brocklehurst, Tony, 1982. Mixed media. Artist's Collection.

A group of squatters who lived opposite Jo Brocklehurst also
became her models. Here, Tony wears a customized leather
jacket and pink leopard-print leggings.

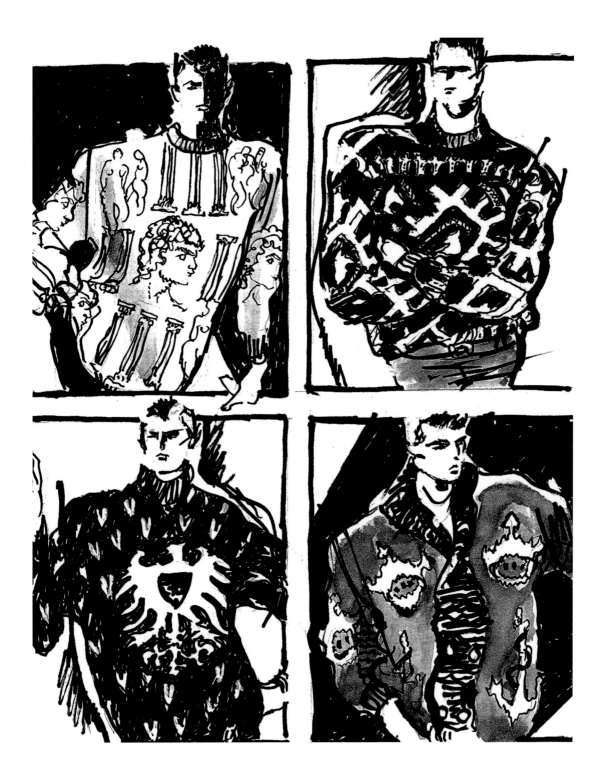

Beryl Hartland, Men's knitwear editorial for the *Daily Telegraph*, mid-1980s. Artist's Collection.

From the 1970s knitwear enjoyed a surge in popularity due to the interest in authentic handmade goods by individual craftsmen. The boom lasted until cheap Third World labour undercut costs in the late 1980s.

Robert Melendez, Original illustration for *Women's Wear Daily*, 1980s. Charcoal on charcoal paper. Artist's Collection.

A chunky charm necklace and upswept hairstyle by Melendez. This drawing was used for the cover of a *Bumble & Bumble* exhibition catalogue in New York in 2006. Melendez was one of *WWD*'s long-term staff illustrators.

Shari Peacock, Vivienne Westwood Punkature collection, 1983.
Watercolour. Private Collection.

Shari Peacock trained as an architect and went on to teach
illustration at Central Saint Martins, London. Her semi-
autobiographical novel, *English as a Foreign Language*, was
published in Bulgaria in 1998, a year before her early death.
Her loose, relaxed style complements Westwood's
unstructured garments.

Shari Peacock, Vivienne Westwood Punkature collection, 1983.
Watercolour. Private Collection.

From Spring 1983 Westwood began to show in Paris. One of the
major conduits of street fashion to the catwalk, she fused many
styles, including multilayered ethnic and historical influences,
underwear as outerwear, workwear and subversive street style.
Her approach remains influential.

Antonio Lopez, Original illustration for cover of *Vanity*,
No. 9, 1983. Pencil, watercolour and gouache on paper.
Courtesy Galerie Bartsch & Chariau, Munich.

A monumental head overwhelms two barely visible figures
in Antonio's homage to Cubism. Maria Snyder, a jewellery
designer, models a Cynzia Ruggieri design.

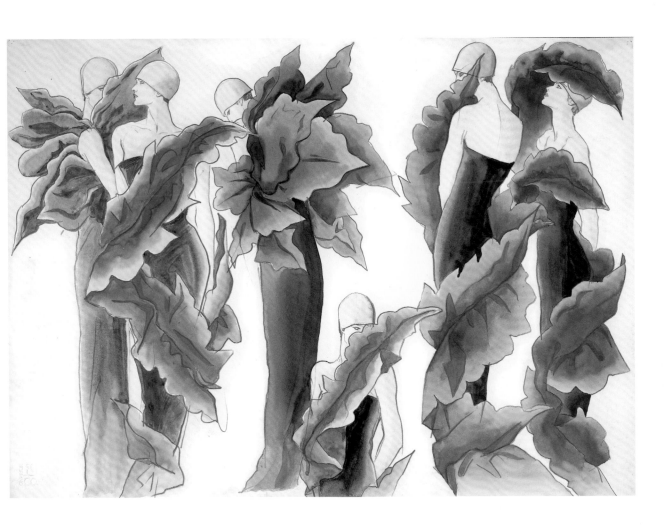

Antonio Lopez, Capucci. Original illustration for *Vanity*, No. 7, 1983. Pencil and watercolour on paper. Courtesy Galerie Bartsch & Chariau, Munich.

Antonio brings his customary fresh approach to this illustration of Capucci's floating, serrated scarves in deep, vibrant colours.

"I'M OF THE OPINION THAT WE SHOULD HAVE TAKEN THE SECOND LEFT OUT OF CASTLE DOUGLAS" GROWLED JOYCE

Glen Baxter, 'Onward into Winter'. Original illustration for British *Vogue*, December 1984. Pen and crayon. Artist's Collection.

Glen Baxter is well known for his humorous drawings with incongruous, witty captions. Fashion has always provided a rich source of material for caricature in publications such as *Punch*.

AS RUNNER-UP IN THE ICE QUEEN CONTEST, EDNA WAS ABOUT TO ENSURE THAT THE WINNER RECEIVED HER PRIZE WITHOUT DELAY

Glen Baxter, 'Onward into Winter'. Original illustration for British *Vogue*, December 1984. Pen and crayon. Artist's Collection.

Knitwear, tweeds and corduroy separates are given a nostalgic interpretation by Baxter, who exhibits internationally and has published numerous books of his cartoons, including such titles as *The Impending Gleam* and *Loomings over the Suet*.

Robert Passantino, Original illustration of sportswear for
Women's Wear Daily, 1984. Rapidograph and marker on vellum.
Artist's Collection.

The craze for aerobics and exercise increased in the 1980s,
accelerating the absorption of sportswear into the fashionable
wardrobe that had started in the late 19th century.

WD ACCESSORIES COVER · 1984   PASSANTINO

Robert Passantino, Original illustration of accessories for
Women's Wear Daily, 1984. Rapidograph, airbrush and crayon
on vellum. Artist's Collection.

A scarf, wide belt and hat are worn with a loose top in
Passantino's illustration for a special accessories issue of *WWD*.

Hat by Stephen Jones - 1985

Pierre Le Tan, Original illustration of hat by Stephen Jones
for *Madame Figaro*, 1985. Ink and watercolour. Courtesy Galerie
Bartsch & Chariau, Munich.

Pierre Le Tan has illustrated for most of the major fashion
magazines, as well as for *The New Yorker* and the *New York Times*.
He now concentrates on writing and illustrating books.
The milliner Stephen Jones is closely associated with John
Galliano at Dior.

Pierre Le Tan, Original illustration of hat by Chloé for
La Mode en peinture, 1982. Ink and watercolour. Courtesy Galerie
Bartsch & Chariau, Munich.

Producing luxury ready-to-wear, the House of Chloé has
employed a succession of head designers, including Karl
Lagerfeld, Martine Sitbon, Stella McCartney and Phoebe Philo.

François Berthoud, Original illustration of Jean-Paul Gaultier
for *Vanity*, 1986. Linocut and watercolour. Courtesy Galerie
Bartsch & Chariau, Munich.

The angular pose and flat rendition of the figure, animal and floral
motifs express the values of Gaultier's 1986 collection, inspired
by Russian Constructivism.

François Berthoud, Original illustration of Jean-Paul Gaultier
for *Vanity*, 1986. Linocut and watercolour. Courtesy Galerie
Bartsch & Chariau, Munich.

Gaultier, often described as the *enfant terrible* of Parisian couture,
launched his first collection in 1976 and has gone on to explore
a multitude of sources in his work.

René Gruau, Original illustration, Capeline Yves Saint Laurent
for *Madame Figaro*, 1986. Ink and watercolour. Courtesy Galerie
Bartsch & Chariau, Munich.

The trend for glamorous dressing-up during the 1980s invested
accessories, especially hats, with a new importance. Saint
Laurent frames the head with a black halo.

René Gruau, Original illustration of Christian Lacroix for cover
of *Madame Figaro*, 1990. Ink and watercolour. Courtesy Galerie
Bartsch & Chariau, Munich.

With only a few brushstrokes, Gruau's energy and verve still shine
through. Lacroix launched his first Paris collection in 1987 and
is known for his use of elaborate surface decoration, combining
colour and pattern, although Gruau chooses not to depict this.

François Berthoud, Original illustration for cover of *Vanity*, 1987.
Coloured linocut. Courtesy The Zahm Collection, Germany.

Berthoud was a major contributor to *Vanity* magazine, illustrating
many of the covers, including this humorous take on Gaultier's
pointed bra.

François Berthoud, Original illustration of Jean-Paul Gaultier
for *Vanity*, 1987. Coloured linocut. Courtesy The Zahm
Collection, Germany.

Gaultier derives much of the inspiration for his work from
subcultural fashion, particularly the London club scene of the
1980s. He continues to push the boundaries of couture, exploring
concepts of gender and sexual ambiguity, which he combines
with classic tailoring and relatively inexpensive fabrics such
as denim, rubber and nylon.

Joe Eula, Original illustration
of Mondi for *W* USA, 1987.
Watercolour. Courtesy The Zahm
Collection, Germany.

A German fashion brand launched
in 1967, Mondi's designs exemplify
1980s 'soft power dressing'.
An American, Joe Eula began his
career in the 1950s. He illustrated
for the *Herald Tribune*, *Life*, the
Sunday Times, *Vogue* and *Harper's
Bazaar*, as well as designing sets
and costumes for the ballet and
theatre. He also collaborated with
Diana Vreeland on exhibitions
at the Metropolitan Museum
of Art, New York.

Claire Smalley, Promotional material for John Galliano, 1987.
Private Collection.

Claire Smalley, a graduate of Central Saint Martins, continued
its ethos of drawing from life. Her lyrical style gives the model
equal importance to the garments and reflects her exacting
preparation. Smalley collaborated closely with Galliano and
later worked for *View*, a forecasting magazine.

Claire Smalley, Promotional material for John Galliano, 1987.
Private Collection.

In 1983 Galliano's graduation collection from Central Saint Martins,
'Les Incroyables', brought him critical acclaim, and in 1987
he won the first of four British Designer of the Year awards.
He went on to head the house of Givenchy and, from 1996,
has been chief designer at Dior.

Claire Smalley, Promotional material for John Galliano, 1987.
Private Collection.

Galliano draws much of his inspiration from historical sources,
but always produces clothes with a glamorous and contemporary
edge. Smalley's graceful models capture the essence of his
essentially romantic style.

Claire Smalley, Promotional material for John Galliano, 1987.
Private Collection.

Smalley's ability to show different textures in her monochrome
drawings provides detail of cut and construction without losing
any of their supreme elegance.

Ty Wilson, Promotional material for Albert Nipon, 1988.
Artist's Collection.

Ty Wilson began his career in New York in the early 1980s.
He has illustrated for many of the major fashion magazines,
including *Vogue*, *WWD*, *Harper's Bazaar* and *Vanity Fair*,
and has done advertising campaigns for Bloomingdale's
and Macy's.

Ty Wilson, Promotional material for Albert Nipon, 1988.
Artist's Collection.

Wilson's ability to convey a sense of movement enhances
the simple shapes of the garments. Originally specializing
in maternity wear, Albert Nipon was Philadelphia's most
famous fashion label from the early 1970s.

Ruben Toledo, 'Gossip in the Dressing Room'. Original illustration for the *New York Times*, 1988. India ink on paper. Artist's Collection.

Cuban artist Ruben Toledo's muse is his fashion designer wife, Isabel, with whom he collaborates closely. Both humorous and informative, this advertisement announced the arrival of the Isabel Toledo lingerie and nightwear collection at Barneys, New York.

Ruben Toledo, 'Ready to Wear Sleepwear'. Original illustration for *Paper Magazine*, 1989. Watercolour on paper. Artist's Collection.

How to layer, reuse and recycle, by Isabel Toledo, for an article on multi-use garments.

Ruben Alterio, Original illustration for *Mirabella* USA, *c*.1989.
Crayon and oil on paper. Courtesy Galerie Bartsch
& Chariau, Munich.

Since the early 1980s the Argentine illustrator Ruben Alterio
has contributed to numerous fashion magazines and has
many corporate clients.

Ruben Alterio, Original illustration for cover of *La Mode en peinture*, 1989. Crayon and oil on paper. Courtesy Galerie Bartsch & Chariau, Munich.

Published from 1982 for ten years, *La Mode en peinture* contributed to the revival in illustration during the period.

ZOLTAN+, Romeo Gigli for *Donna*, 1993. Artist's Collection.

Romeo Gigli showed his first collection in 1983, designing
romantic clothes in rich colours and textures wrapped around
the body with a soft silhouette. Zoltan, an Hungarian artist,
also collaborated with Issey Miyake and illustrated numerous
fashion magazines before moving on to photography
and computer graphics.

ZOLTAN+, Yohji Yamamoto for *Femme*, 1989. Artist's Collection.

Yamamoto was at the forefront of the avant-garde Japanese designers who started to show in Paris in the 1980s. Their intellectual approach, embodied in layered, figure-concealing garments, was the antithesis to 1980s 'power dressing' and was to transform fashion during this period.

Hirshleifer's *men*

Ty Wilson, Paul Costelloe, 1990. Artist's Collection.

Irish-born designer Paul Costelloe established his own label in 1979. His trademarks are comfortable classics in natural fabrics – fluid linens, tweeds, cashmere and leather.

Ty Wilson, Promotional material for Hirshleifer's, 1990. Artist's Collection.

Ty Wilson's swaggering style captures the soft, yet exaggerated silhouette of early 1990s menswear.

KENNETH PAUL BLOCK
A RETROSPECTIVE

JUNE 2 - 26, 1999
SOCIETY of ILLUSTRATORS
MUSEUM of AMERICAN ILLUSTRATION

Kenneth Paul Block, Cover of catalogue for exhibition, 1999.
Private Collection.

Trained at Parsons School of Art and Design, New York, Kenneth
Paul Block was the best known of the illustrators at *WWD*. His
career spanned the period when fashion illustration was under
threat and he is considered to be pivotal in its eventual survival.

Michael Roberts, Azzedine Alaïa, 'Sphinx dress', for *The Sunday Times*, March 1990. Paper collage. Courtesy Artist's Collection / Maconochie Photography.

Michael Roberts' ironic style is mediated through the laborious technique of paper mosaic collage. An iconic stylist, photographer and fashion editor, he creates illustrations that are uniquely daring and reflect his own individuality.

Michael Roberts, Azzedine Alaïa, 'Fringed skirt', for *The Sunday Times*, March 1990. Paper collage. Courtesy Artist's Collection/Maconochie Photography.

The Tunisian designer Azzedine Alaïa, known as 'the king of cling', uses Lycra, leather and zips to create body-hugging designs that are simultaneously provocative and elegant.

Ruben Toledo, 'Santo Mugler' and 'Santo Alaïa', *Visionaire*, 'Heaven' issue, December 1991. Courtesy *Visionaire*.

Visionaire, launched in 1991, publishes three themed issues a year and continually pushes the boundaries of illustration. The 'Heaven' issue contained images elevating designers to the status of sainthood.

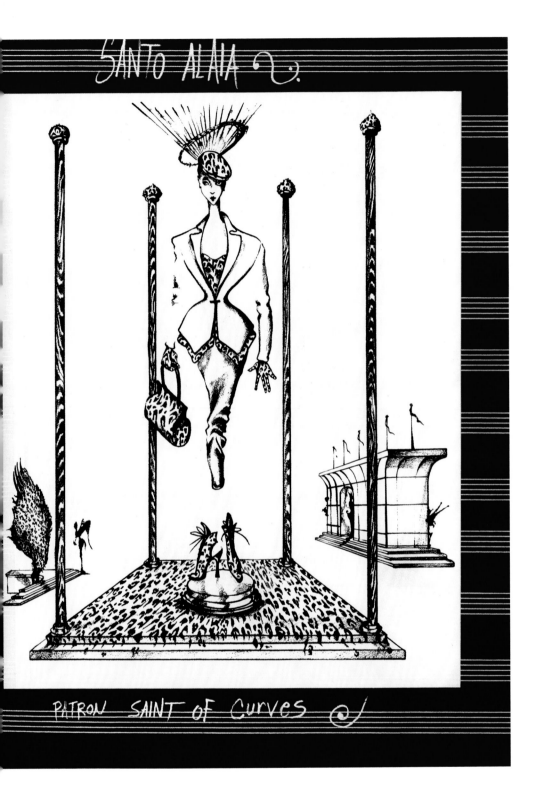

SANTO ALAIA

PATRON SAINT OF CURVES

Steven Stipelman, Evening gown for *Women's Wear Daily*, 1991.
Artist's Collection.

A white, cloud-like evening gown floats against a dark ground
in Stipelman's 'mood' illustration.

Ruben Toledo, 'Under the Veil'. Original illustration for *Vogue Nippon*, 1992. Watercolour on paper. Artist's Collection.

Isabel Toledo's Under the Veil collection featured mermaid-like sheath dresses in velvet and silk chiffon.

Un coup de dés jamais n'abolira le hasard

Mallarmé

Christian Dior

ZOLTAN+, Christian Dior for Comité Montaigne / French *Vogue*,
1992. Artist's Collection.

At this time Gianfranco Ferre was head designer at Christian Dior.
Zoltan often used, as he does here, a combination of illustration,
collage and photography.

Cartier

ZOLTAN+, Cartier for Comité Montaigne / French *Vogue*, 1992.
Artist's Collection.

Founded in 1847, the Maison Cartier has remained at the forefront
of luxury jewellery, perhaps best known for its animal designs,
such as this panther in platinum, diamonds and sapphires.

Patrick Arlet, Orignal illustration for *Marie Claire* France, *c.*1992.
Oil on paper. Courtesy Galerie Bartsch & Chariau, Munich.

A face-framing hat and bow cravat feature in Arlet's
dramatic illustration.

Patrick Arlet, Rifat Ozbek. Original illustration for
Marie Claire France, *c.*1992. Oil on cardboard.
Courtesy Galerie Bartsch & Chariau, Munich.

Rifat Ozbek clothes the 'modern nomad', drawing inspiration
from his own (Turkish) cultural heritage, from other ethnic textile
and decorative traditions, and from the London club scene.
Here the formality of a tailcoat is contrasted with a man's shirt
and track pants.

BLACK LEATHER: VIVIENNE WESTWOOD WINTER 91/92

Gladys Perint Palmer, Vivienne Westwood, Winter 1991/2,
for *Grazia* Italy, November 1991. Mixed media on paper.
Courtesy V&A Images.

A black leather cropped jacket, platform thigh boots and
suspenders continue Westwood's exploration of fetish wear.
Gladys Perint Palmer has done illustrations for all the major
fashion magazines and for many designers' campaigns.
She has exhibited widely and is currently Executive Director
of Fashion at Academy of Art University, San Francisco.

Gladys Perint Palmer, Vivienne Westwood, Winter 1993.
Mixed media on paper. Courtesy V&A Images.

Palmer brings a lively humour to her work, capturing the essence
of Westwood's anarchic Anglomania collection, which gave
a distinctly contemporary flavour to traditional Scottish textiles
such as mohair tartan and Argyll knit. The outrageously high
platform pumps complete the sartorial pun.

Jo Brocklehurst, Izzy in club wear, early 1990s. Mixed media.
Artist's Collection.

An outfit of body armour called 'Way of the Wyrd', made by
Anthony Gregory out of a steel framework, worn over a Lycra
bodysuit at the 'Rubber Ball', an annual celebration of fetish
wear at Hammersmith Palais, London.

Jo Brocklehurst, Rasta Mary in club wear, 1994. Mixed media.
Artist's Collection.

Brocklehurst's dazzling drawing of Rasta Mary in her outfit
for the 'Rubber Ball' (see opposite). Mary was the manageress
of Boy, a boutique in the King's Road, London, which supplied
a mix of secondhand and glam rock club wear.

François Berthoud, Chloé, 1994. Linocut and monotype.
Courtesy Galerie Bartsch & Chariau, Munich.

A filigree silhouette epitomizes Berthoud's combination
of delicacy and strength.

François Berthoud, Wire dummy, 1994. Linocut and monotype.
Courtesy Galerie Bartsch & Chariau, Munich.

Perhaps in an ironic comment, Berthoud's wire dummy expresses
the ultimate emptiness of the world of fashion, but also references
Jean-Paul Gaultier's 1989 'Wedding Cage' dress.

Robert Passantino, Man with Head. Original illustration for
the *Daily News Record*, 1994. Brush, acrylic, ink and collage.
Artist's Collection.

In a special article on men's toiletries, Passantino combines
collage and painting.

Robert Passantino, Tarzan. Original illustration for
the *Daily News Record*, 1994. Brush, acrylic, ink and collage.
Artist's Collection.

Men's cosmetics have become big business and here Tarzan
looks exceptionally well groomed.

Kareem Iliya, Ann Demeulemeester for *Visionaire*,
'White' Issue, 1994. Artist's Collection.

One of the 'Antwerp Six', Demeulemeester is a deconstructionist
who layers and drapes textured and antiqued fabrics, sometimes
with raw edges, into a subtle mix of couture and subcultural
elements. Lebanese-born Iliya is a graduate of the Fashion
Institute of Technology, New York, and has concentrated on
illustration since 1992. Using a bleeding technique, he creates
halos of suffused colour on and around his subject.

Steven Stipelman, Black dress, 1996. Artist's Collection.

Continual experimentation and exploration of different types
of media are vital for the development of an artist's work. In this
personal (rather than commissioned) work, Stipelman conveys
the effect of layers of sheer, spotted fabric.

Mats Gustafson, Original illustration of Prada for Italian *Vogue*,
1997. Watercolour. Artist's Collection.

Since the late 1970s, Mats Gustafson, who trained as a costume
designer at the Scandinavian Drama Institute, Stockholm,
has had his work published in all the major fashion magazines.
His diffused, shadowy images create an atmosphere and mood
that are unique.

Mats Gustafson, Original illustration of Prada for Italian *Vogue*,
1997. Watercolour. Artist's Collection.

Transforming an old family firm into a global conglomerate,
Miuccia Prada has established a reputation for understated
clothes and accessories that are immediately recognizable
to the fashion cognoscenti.

Mats Gustafson, Original illustration of Comme des Garçons for Italian *Vogue*, 1997. Pastel and chalk. Artist's Collection.

Rei Kawakubo founded Comme des Garçons in Japan in 1969 and began showing in Paris in the early 1980s. Her work is distinguished by its warped asymmetry, distressed fabrics and monochrome palette.

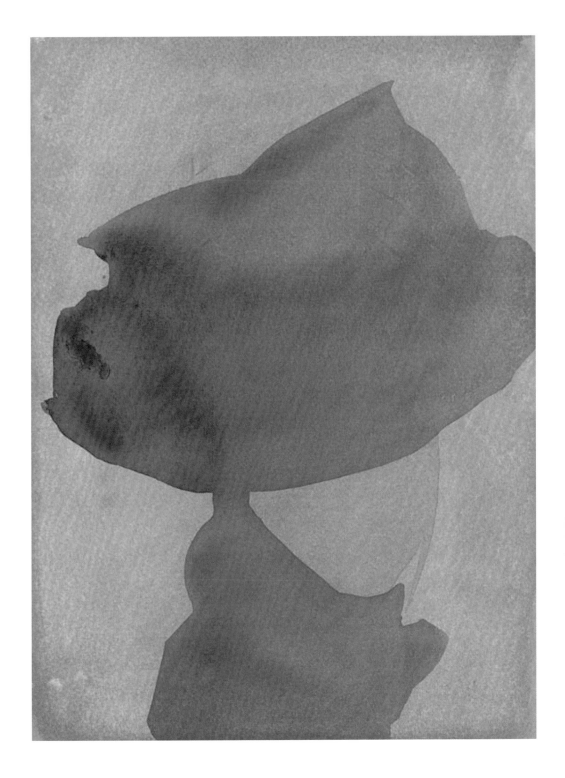

Mats Gustafson, Original illustration of Yohji Yamamoto for *Vogue Nippon*, 1998. Watercolour. Artist's Collection.

Mats rarely gives his fashion models a visual identity, though this did not prevent the Council of Fashion Designers of America from commissioning him to do a series of portraits of designers honoured by them.

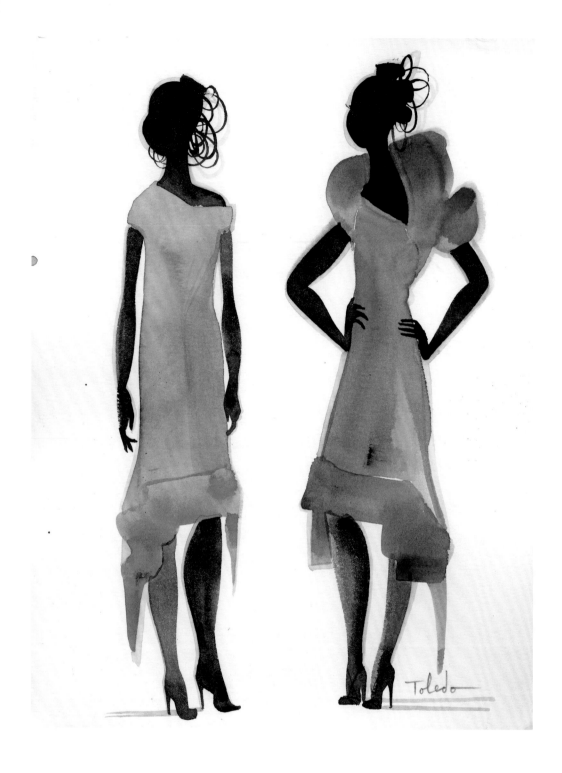

Ruben Toledo, 'Black Magic from Cuba'. Original illustration for
French *Vogue*, 1997. India ink and watercolour on paper.
Artist's Collection.

Inspired by a trip to Cuba, Toledo uses black models to show
asymmetrical necklines and handkerchief-point hemlines
in contrasting colour.

Ruben Toledo, 'Mug Shot Lineup'. Original illustration, 1998.
Watercolour on paper. Artist's Collection.

Fabric wrapped and draped around the torso softens
the line of the hobble skirts. Ruben Toledo's illustration was
used for a poster advertising a retrospective exhibition
of the work of his wife, Isabel Toledo, at the Fashion Institute
of Technology, New York.

Robert Melendez, Original illustration of swimwear for
Women's Wear Daily, 1999. Artist's Collection.

Trained at Parsons School in New York, Melendez imbues
his swimwear with glamour and glitz in a promotional calendar.
As well as *WWD*, he illustrated for the *New York Times*, the *Daily
News Record* and Saks Fifth Avenue from the 1970s.

Robert Melendez, Original illustration of suit for *Women's Wear Daily*, 1999. Artist's Collection.

Melendez's drawing of a 1940s-style suit with pillbox hat and veil combines accurate detail with wit and attitude.

Tanya Ling, Original illustration for US *Elle* Trend Report,
Fall/Winter 2000. Mixed media on paper. Artist's Collection.

Forecasting future trends is an important facet of the fashion
industry, and by its very nature is most suitable for interpretation
through illustration. Here, Tanya Ling, an artist and designer who
has gone on to specialize in illustration, depicts a dress with
black bodice and frothy, dotted skirt.

Tanya Ling, Original illustration of Boudicca, Spring/Summer
2001 for *Paper*, December 2000. Mixed media on coloured paper.
Artist's Collection.

Boudicca, a label launched in 1997, has become known for
its conceptual approach to precision tailoring. This illustration
was featured on the back cover of a booklet for *Paper* magazine
called 'A Fashion Odyssey'.

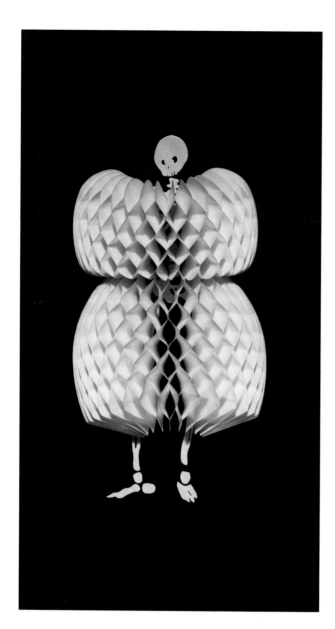

François Berthoud, Junya Watanabe, *Visionaire*, 'Touch' issue, October 2000. Courtesy *Visionaire*.

Concertina-folded paper dresses a skeleton in Berthoud's innovative illustration.

François Berthoud, Yohji Yamamoto, *Visionaire*, 'Touch' issue, October 2000. Courtesy *Visionaire*.

Fur collaged onto a figure expresses perfectly the theme of *Visionaire*'s 'Touch' issue.

Kareem Iliya, Original illustration of Prada for *Chicago Tribune*, 2001. Artist's Collection.

An explosion of diffused colour highlights the simplicity of Prada's monochrome ensemble.

Howard Tangye, Emma in Chloé, *c.*2001.
Artist's Collection.

A vintage Chloé dress drawn by Howard Tangye,
a passionate believer in the importance of life drawing
combined with continuous practice. His illustrations
are infused with a lyrical sensitivity.

Chloé dress, British *Vogue*, April 1967. Courtesy The Condé
Nast Publications Ltd/Photograph David Montgomery.

In 1967 *Vogue* highlighted the influence of Aubrey Beardsley's
work by featuring the Chloé original (see opposite) printed with
Beardsleyesque motifs. The V&A held an exhibition of his work
in 1966.

David Remfry, Stella McCartney, 2002. Graphite and wash on paper. (Collection of V&A Museum, Purchase 2004.) Courtesy the Artist.

Stella McCartney revitalized the House of Chloé when she was appointed creative director in 1997. Since launching her own label in 2001 in collaboration with the Gucci group, she has continued to design edgy, feminine clothes with a wide appeal.

David Remfry, Stella McCartney, 2002. Graphite and wash
on paper. (Collection of V&A Museum, Purchase 2004.)
Courtesy the Artist.

David Remfry, a British artist who has exhibited extensively,
was commissioned by McCartney to produce a series of drawings
for her first advertising campaign and her campaign for Absolut
Vodka. He captures her signature look of erotic cool, embodied
by model Tatyana.

David Downton, Portrait of Anna Piaggi, 2001. Oil pastel,
gouache and ink on Pantone paper and acetate overlay.
Artist's Collection.

Downton's portrait of Anna Piaggi, drawn between Paris catwalk
shows, captures the spirit and eccentric chic of the Italian fashion
editor, the subject of an exhibition at the V&A in 2006.

David Downton, Portrait of Amanda Harlech, *Telegraph Magazine*, July 2002. Ink, pastel and gouache on paper. Artist's Collection.

A former fashion editor at *Harper's and Queen*, Amanda, Lady Harlech, became Karl Lagerfeld's inspirational muse in 1997. Drawn by Downton in her suite at the Paris Ritz, she epitomizes the easy elegance perennially associated with the House of Chanel.

François Berthoud, Original illustration for *Architectural Digest*
France, 2002. Linocut and monotype on paper. Courtesy Galerie
Bartsch & Chariau, Munich.

Berthoud's image is reduced to a monumental minimum.

François Berthoud, Original illustration for Burberrys, 2003.
Linocut and monotype on paper. Courtesy Galerie Bartsch
& Chariau, Munich.

Burberrys continues to produce British classics. The coat is lined
with the company's signature checked fabric.

ZOLTAN+

ZOLTAN+, Balmain couture mask for *DNA* magazine, 2003.
Artist's Collection.

The House of Balmain opened in 1945 and retains its position
at the heart of prestigious couture.

ZOLTAN+, Couture for *Double* magazine, 2003.
Artist's Collection.

Zoltan's powerfully strident figure expresses the inspiration
he took from the 2003 Paris collections.

Jean-Philippe Delhomme, Original illustration of Christian
Lacroix for *Madame Figaro*, 2003. Artist's Collection.

Christian Lacroix at work in his atelier.

Jean-Philippe Delhomme, Original illustration of Galliano
catwalk show for *Madame Figaro*, 2003. Artist's Collection.

John Galliano's shows are known for their spectacular themes
and settings.

100

Piet Paris, Shawl 1, 2003. Artist's Collection.

Trained at the Academy of Fine Arts in Arnhem, Piet Paris is one
of the best-known Dutch illustrators, working for many magazines,
for *De Telegraaf* and for corporate clients.

COLLECTIE NAJAAR 2003

Piet Paris, Najaar, 2003. Artist's Collection.

Often using stencils and a paint roller, Paris reduces the figure
and garments to a stylized minimum.

Jason Brooks, Versace for *Vogue pelle*, 2003.
Pen, ink and Adobe Photoshop. Artist's Collection.

Jason Brooks was one of the first fashion illustrators
to explore the potential of computer graphics.
Versace's psychedelic print minidress is idiomatic of the
1960s, but the computer-generated image, the styling
and the accessories are unmistakably 21st century.

Jason Brooks, Chanel, 2004. Pen, ink and Adobe Photoshop.
Artist's Collection.

A white minidress and boots by Chanel are accessorized
with black stockings and a diamond necklace. Since 1983
the charismatic Karl Lagerfeld has been chief designer
for the House of Chanel.

David Downton, Advertisement for TopShop's Atelier collection,
September 2004. Dr Martin's ink and gouache on paper.
Artist's Collection.

Frequently depicted by David Downton, model Erin O'Connor
poses in TopShop's Atelier couture range. The store has
consistently produced up-to-the-minute styles at high-street
prices, as well as supporting young designers.

David Downton, Original illustration of Christian Lacroix
for *V Magazine* USA, July 2004. Gouache and ink on paper.
Artist's Collection.

Supermodel Linda Evangelista wears Christian Lacroix.
Downton's superb draughtsmanship never gets in the way
of depicting the clothes in detail. This was done during
a seven-hour sitting at the Hotel George V in Paris, with makeup
artist, hairdresser and stylist in attendance – as Downton says,
'A total luxury: fashion illustration as it once was.'

Liselotte Watkins, Martin Bergström for *Vive la Suède*,
Swedish online magazine, January 2004. Adobe Photoshop.
Artist's Collection.

Liselotte Watkins represents a new generation of young
Swedish illustrators. Her colourful work is filled with vibrant
texture and pattern.

Liselotte Watkins, Martin Bergström for *Vive la Suède*,
Swedish online magazine, January 2004. Adobe Photoshop.
Artist's Collection.

Bergström is a Swedish designer who produces handmade
garments, mostly for private clients.

Gladys Perint Palmer, Dior for *L'Officiel* Russia, December 2004.
Artist's Collection.

Galliano's Autumn/Winter collection 2004 for Dior was inspired
by a trip to Vienna. Hungarian-born Perint Palmer here evokes the
spirit of the Empress Elisabeth and the *fin-de-siècle* extravagance
of the Austro-Hungarian empire.

Grayson Perry, Christian Lacroix for *Spoon*, Summer 2005.
Courtesy *Spoon* magazine.

Commissioned by *Spoon* magazine in July 2005 to report on the
Paris collections, artist and potter Grayson Perry brought a new,
uneasy aesthetic to his fashion illustrations. Here he produces
work that reflects the horror of the London bombings.

Grayson Perry, Chanel for *Spoon*, Summer 2005. Courtesy
Spoon magazine.

Juxtaposing couture with a police appeal for help in solving crime,
Perry underlines the paradoxical relationship between fashion
and issues of social anxiety.

Autumn Whitehurst, Accessories for the *Telegraph Magazine*,
September 2005. Adobe Photoshop and Adobe Illustrator.
Artist's Collection.

A variety of accessories by Clements Ribeiro, Prada and Chanel
are depicted in Whitehurst's whimsical, hyper-realistic style.

Autumn Whitehurst, Accessories for the *Telegraph Magazine*,
September 2005. Adobe Photoshop and Adobe Illustrator.
Artist's Collection.

Fur-lined boots by Gucci, rose corsage by Dries van Noten and
a gold chain necklace by Marc Jacobs. Whitehurst's aim was
to make the images 'look as though these girls raided some
God-sent armoire full of accessories with which to fantasize in'.

Kareem Iliya, Postcard for Saks Fifth Avenue, 2005.
Artist's Collection.

Iliya's illustration is suffused with atmospheric colour.

FURTHER READING

Backmeyer, S (ed)., *Picture This: The Artist as Illustrator*, Central Saint Martins in association with The Herbert Press, London, 2005

Barnes, C., *Fashion Illustration*, Little, Brown, London, 1994

Borrelli, L., *Fashion Illustration Next*, Thames & Hudson, London, 2004

Borrelli, L., *Fashion Illustration Now*, Thames & Hudson, London, 2000

Braithwaite, B., *Women's Magazines: The First 300 Years*, Peter Owen, London, 1995

Breward, C., *Fashion*, Oxford University Press, Oxford, 2003

Bryant, M W., *WWD Illustrated*, Fairchild, New York, 2004

Chase, E W., *Always in Vogue*, Garden City, USA, 1954

Dancyger, I., *A World of Women: An Illustrated History of Women's Magazines*, Gill & Macmillan, Dublin, 1978

Dawber, M., *Imagemakers: Cutting Edge Fashion Illustration*, Mitchell Beazley, London, 2004

Dawber, M., *New Fashion Illustration*, Batsford, London, 2005

Drake, N., *Fashion Illustration Today*, Thames & Hudson, London, 1994

Drake, N., *French Fashion Plates from the Gazette du bon ton*, Dover, New York, 1979

Erté, *Designs by Erté: Fashion Drawings and Illustrations from Harper's Bazaar*, Constable, London; Dover, New York, 1976

Ferguson, M., *Forever Feminine: Women's Magazines and the Cult of Femininity*, Gower, Aldershot, UK, 1983

Ginsburg, M., *An Introduction to Fashion Illustration*, V&A Publications, London, 1980

Lepape, C., Defert, T., *From the Ballets Russes to Vogue: The Art of Georges Lepape*, Thames & Hudson, London, 1984

Lopez, A., *60 70 80: Three Decades of Fashion Illustration*, Thames & Hudson, London, 1995

Moore, D L., *Fashion through Fashion Plates 1771–1970*, Ward Lock, London, 1971

Packer, W., *Fashion Drawing in Vogue*, Coward McCann, New York, 1983

Perint Palmer, G., *Fashion People*, Assouline, New York, 2003

Robinson, J., *The Fine Art of Fashion: An Illustrated History*, Bay Books, New South Wales, 1989

Robinson, J., *The Golden Age of Style: Art Deco Fashion Illustration*, Orbis, London, 1976

Seebohm, C., *The Man who was Vogue: The Life and Times of Condé Nast*, Weidenfield & Nicolson, London, 1982

Steele, V., *Paris Fashion: A Cultural History*, Oxford University Press, New York and Oxford, 1988

Vittu, F et al., *Dessins sous toutes ses coutures: croquis, illustrations, modèles 1760–1994*, Paris-Musées, Paris, 1995

White, C., *Women's Magazines 1693–1968*, Joseph, London, 1970

Zahm, V (ed)., *Art Fashion: Original Works of Famous 20th Century Fashion Illustrators from the Collection Volker & Ingrid Zahm*, Zahm, Germany 1994

LIST OF ILLUSTRATORS

Page numbers in italics refer to illustrations.

PICTURE CREDITS

The publishers wish to thank the institutions and individuals who have kindly provided photographic materials for use in this book. In all cases, every effort has been made to contact the copyright holders, but should there be any errors or omissions the publishers would be pleased to insert the appropriate acknowledgement in any subsequent edition of this book.

© ADAGP, Paris and DACS, London 2006: pp. 18 right, 19, 20, 21, 22 left, 30 left, 30 right, 34, 35, 36, 37, 38, 39, 41, bottom, 45, 48, 49, 51 left & right, 71, 82, 119, 122 left & right, 123, 132, 133, 148, 152. © Ruben Alterio: pp. 260, 304, 305. © Patrick Arlet: pp. 320, 321. © Sylvia Ayton: p. 229. © Glen Baxter: pp. 284, 285. © François Berthoud: pp. 290, 291, 294, 295, 328, 329, 348 left & right, 358, 359 © Bibliothèque des Arts Decoratifs, Paris, France: p. 41 top. © Celia Birtwell: pp. 228, 244, 245. © Kenneth Paul Block: p. 309. © Mr.Matrand de La Bourdonnaye Blossac: pp. 162, 163, 171. © The Trustees of the British Museum: p. 6. © Jo Brocklehurst: pp. 276, 277, 326, 327. © Jason Brooks: p. 261, 366, 367. © Paul Caranicas: pp. 236, 237, 248, 249, 252, 253, 270, 271, 282, 283. © The Condé Nast Archive: pp. 88, 89, 102, 103, 106, 107, 110, 111, 112, 113, 114, 120 Alfredo Bouret/Vogue © The Condé Nast Publications Ltd.: pp. 194, 195 Eric/Vogue © The Condé Nast Publications Ltd.: pp. 73, 118. © David Montgomery/Vogue. © The Condé Nast Publications Ltd.: p. 353. © DACS 2006: pp. 67, 87, 166, 183, 191, 192, 193, 220, 230, 231. © Jean-Philippe Delhomme: pp. 324, 325, 362, 363. © David Downton: pp. 342, 343, 356, 357, 368, 369. © Joe Eula: pp. 296, 297. © The Fine Art Society, London, UK: p. 18 left. © Fitzwilliam Museum, University of Cambridge, UK: p. 9. © The Family of the late Eric Fraser: p. 80. © www.renegruau.com: pp. 154, 156, 158, 159, 160, 172, 173, 184 left & right, 186, 187, 214, 215, 216, 217, 232, 233, 275, 292, 293. Vogue/The Condé Nast Publications Ltd. © www.renegruau.com: p. 190 right. © Mats Gustafson: pp. 334, 335, 336, 337. © Beryl Hartland: pp. 180, 181, 266 right, 278. © M. Wesel-Henrion: p. 139. © Bobby Hillson: pp. 206 left & right, 222, 223, 239. © Kareem Iliya: pp. 332, 349, 378. © Dietmar Katz: p. 131 right. © Rosalind C. Kimball: pp. 174, 175, 176/177. © L&M SERVICES B.V. Amsterdam 20060613: p. 65 top & bottom. © Angela Landels: p. 207. © Tanya Ling www.tanyaling.com: pp. 344, 345. © Robert Melendez: pp. 279, 340, 341. © Gladys Perint Palmer: pp. 322, 323, 372/373. © Piet Paris: pp. 364, 365. © Robert Passantino: pp. 169, 246, 247, 286, 287, 330, 331. © Grayson Perry: pp. 374, 375. © Kunstbibliothek, SMB/Knud Petersen: pp. 130 right, 131. © David Remfry: pp. 354, 355 © Michael Roberts/Maconochie Photography: p. 310. © Graham Rounthwaite: pp. 346, 347 The Royal Collection © 2006, Her Majesty Queen Elizabeth II: p. 185. © Sevenarts Ltd/DACS 2006: pp. 31 left & right, 95, 108, 115. © Estate of Claire Smalley: pp. 298, 299, 300, 301. © Caroline Smith: pp. 224, 225, 254, 255, 256, 257. © Steven Stipelman: pp. 259 bottom, 267, 274, 316, 333. © Elizabeth Suter: pp. 264 left & right, 265. © Pierre Le Tan: pp. 288, 289. © Howard Tangye: p. 352. © Ruben Toledo: pp. 303 left & right, 312/313, 314/315, 317, 338, 339. © Julie Verhoeven: pp. 350 left & right, 351. © Andy Warhol Foundation: pp. 197, 198, 199, 200, 201, 203. © Liselotte Watkins: pp. 370, 371. © Vivienne Westwood/Vivienne Westwood Archive: p. 259 top. © Autumn Whitehurst: pp. 376, 377. © Ty Wilson.com: pp. 302 left & right, 308. © ZOLTAN+: pp. 306, 307, 318, 319, 360, 361. Photographs © CSM: pp. frontispiece, 8, 30L, 32, 33, 34,35, 36,37, 38, 39, 40, 46, 47, 48,49, 50, 51, 81, 85, 86, 92, 93, 94, 95, 99, 100, 101, 104, 108, 109, 115, 124, 125, 128, 129, 132, 133, 136, 146, 161, 166, 168, 174, 175, 176/177, 180, 181, 182, 186, 187, 206, 212, 213, 216, 217, 218, 219, 222, 223, 226, 227, 229, 239, 240, 241, 242, 243, 264, 265, 268, 269, 276, 277, 280, 281, 284, 285, 298, 299, 300, 301, 309, 326, 327, 352

 The publishers of *100 Years of Fashion Illustration* have paid DACS' visual creators for the use of their artistic works.

ACKNOWLEDGEMENTS

I am deeply indebted to all the artists, past and present, whose work fills the pages of this book. I hope I have done them justice and by doing so, done something to counter the historic marginalization of fashion illustration. As a means of disseminating fashion, it has consistently and unfairly been judged alongside photography; however, its continued survival and recent renaissance stand testament to its value as an important artistic genre and cultural document.

Inevitably, there are numerous illustrators whose work I have not been able to include – for every famous name there are dozens of unsung heroes, often uncredited and unrecognized, whose work enriches the pages of so many publications – and for this, I apologise.

I am grateful to the picture libraries, galleries, archives, museums and individuals whose collections I have plundered, and in the case of many deceased artists, to their copyright holders. I would particularly like to thank the following for their expert help and advice: Madeleine Ginsburg of the DAKS/Simpson Archive, London; Professor Aileen Ribeiro of the Courtauld Institute, London; Christine Isteed of Artist Partners, London; Sonnet Stanfill, Curator of Contemporary Fashion at the Victoria and Albert Museum, London; Rie Nii at the Kyoto Costume Institute, Japan; Liz and Philip de Bay at the Stapleton Collection, London; Joelle Chariau and Andreas Bartsch at Galerie Barstch & Chariau, Munich; Herr Volker Zahm and Veronika Peter at the Zahm Collection, Germany; Francoise Vittu at the Palais Galliera, Paris; Janine Button, Nicky Budden and Harriet Wilson at Condé Nast, London; Rosemary Harden and Elly Summers at the Museum of Costume, Bath; Barbara Jeauffroy at Archives Christian Dior, Paris; Madalief Hohe at The Gemeentemuseum, Den Haag, Netherlands; Stephanie Pesakoff at Art Department, New York; Reina Nakagawa at Art and Commerce, New York; Cecilia Dean at Visionaire, New York; Tiggy Maconochie of Maconochie Photography, London; Taiko Hasegawa at Taiko Associates, Japan; Joshua Waller at the Fashion Institute of Technology, New York; Red Harty at Spoon Magazine, London; William Ling; Constance Wibaut; Izzy.

At Central Saint Martins I would like to thank Catherine Pound and Sylvia Backmeyer of the Archive for their generous help; Tim Marshall for his photography; Dani Salvadori and Ishbel Neat of the Innovation Centre; Peter Close, School Administrator; and my colleagues Rebecca Arnold, Megumi Ohki, Howard Tangye and Judith Watt. At the London College of Fashion, Heather Lambert and Katherine Baird.

I am very grateful for Anne Townley's kindness and patience as editor at Laurence King; for Claire Gouldstone's unfailing help through difficult times for us both; and to Alice Peebles and David Tanguy who have helped to make the book what it is.

Thanks to Bonnie and Ophelia Blackman, and to Mary Grimsditch, Rose Hepworth, Simon Wood, Lidy Trompetter and Kiempe Reitsma, and also to Marion Treasure who photographed many of the illustrations and, as always, lived up to her name.

My greatest debt of gratitude is to my husband, Glen, who got me through – thank you.